'With a clever premise, fun and lively text, and a particularly brilliant story about Abram that I have never before seen retold, Krish and Miriam Kandiah have created a terrific book that celebrates the diversity of people and cultures found in the Bible.'

Bob Hartman, bestselling children's author

'Miriam and Krish take parents, carers and children on an exciting global adventure through the Bible.'

Tim and Rachel Hughes, Lead Pastors at Gas Street Church

'When I was growing up, I thought the Bible consisted of white people, not people who looked like me. This much-needed book by Krish and Miriam will bring joy to so many children as they see themselves reflected in the most famous stories in history. Fun and accessible, yet filled with truth, I hope *Whistlestop Tales* helps to redress the balance for my son and children like him everywhere.'

Chine McDonald, writer, broadcaster and author of God Is Not a White Man

'This book has been a long time coming. Celebrating the cultures in the Bible, placing the stories in their original setting, taking it back to the inclusive place, allows us to recognise that the Bible is full of people just like us.'

Carrie Grant MBE and David Grant MBE

KRISH AND MIRIAM KANDIAH
ILLUSTRATED BY ANDY GRAY

WHISTLESTOP TALES

AROUND THE
WORLD IN
10 BIBLE STORIES

First published in Great Britain in 2021 by Hodder & Stoughton
An Hachette UK company

1

Copyright © Krish and Miriam Kandiah, 2021
Illustrations © Andy S. Gray, Onegraydot Ltd.

A CIP catalogue record for this title is available from the British Library

Hardback ISBN 978 1 529 37753 8
eBook ISBN 978 1 529 37755 2

Typeset by Andy S. Gray, Onegraydot Ltd.

Printed and bound in Great Britain by Clays Ltd, Elcograf S.p.A.

Hodder & Stoughton policy is to use papers that are natural, renewable and recyclable products and made from wood grown in sustainable forests. The logging and manufacturing processes are expected to conform to the environmental regulations of the country of origin.

Hodder & Stoughton Ltd
Carmelite House
50 Victoria Embankment
London EC4Y 0DZ

www.hodderfaithyoungexplorers.co.uk

To our Niblings:
Leo, Zac, Roxy and James.

CONTENTS

Dear Reader,

When I was young, I was the only boy in my class who wasn't white. My mum said it was because I was special, but my classmates didn't see it that way. They bullied me and called me names because I was different. Some of the things they said were really stupid. For example, they kept calling me black, even though my skin was clearly brown. They insisted on saying I was Pakistani even though I had told them hundreds of times that I wasn't. I was British, with an Indian mother and a Sri Lankan father. Perhaps that was too many words for them to turn into an insult. Some of them weren't that clever.

I often looked in books for characters who were not that different from me, but I didn't find any. It wasn't until I was much, much older that I realised the answer had been right under my nose all along. You see, when I was seven years old, I had been given a Bible. Little did I know then that it was full of people from all sorts of places with all sorts of skin shades who had to deal with all sorts of problems. It told stories of adventurers who were African and Middle Eastern and Asian as well as European.

Perhaps it was because the place names had all been different back then that I hadn't understood just how international the Bible was. But some of its characters came from countries I had actually visited, or seen on the news, or read about in other books. If only I had realised this when I was young – those Bible stories might have encouraged me to stand a little taller. If only my classmates had read them too – perhaps they would have been a little kinder.

That's why Miriam and I wrote this book together. We wanted children everywhere to know that inspiring people can come from anywhere. So we worked out where some of our favourite Bible characters would have lived on today's map, and we let them capture our imagination. The following stories may not quite be how the Bible tells them, but I hope they convey one really important, overarching and true message of the Bible: wherever you are from, whatever colour your skin is, whatever people say about you, you can be part of God's global adventure.

Your friend,
Krish

ABRAM

THE TALE OF THE INTREPID IRAQI
WHO HAD A LOT TO LOSE

WELCOME TO IRAQ

Deep below the deserts of Iraq are buried huge
lakes of oil. It might just seem like a lot of sticky
black sludge, but it is, in fact, extremely valuable sticky
black sludge. The Iraqi people extract the oil and then
trade it with other countries in exchange for large amounts
of money and food. Then the oil is turned into useful things
like petrol, and plastics and soaps, although we use a little

too much of those things.

Sadly, the amount of oil we get through each day is beginning to destroy the beautiful world we live in. In this tale, the oil fields are a place to be avoided and one intrepid Iraqi launches a daring raid to extract something that he believed was even more valuable than the sticky black sludge found in the ground.

The campsite was a lot quieter since old Abram's nephew had gone.

The boy's name was Lot, which was a good name for someone who made a lot of noise, got into a lot of trouble and asked a lot of questions.

'Where did I come from again?' Lot used to ask. 'What was Iraq like? Why did we leave? What happened to my parents? Where are we going to? Are we nearly there yet?'

Abram must have tried to answer those questions hundreds of times – usually late at night huddled under a blanket, sipping hot soup by a crackling campfire. Lot loved listening to all his uncle's stories.

But now Lot was gone.

Now there was nobody waking Abram up in the middle

of the night with loud snoring from the tent next door.

There was no one upsetting the other campers with pranks and mishaps.

There was nobody shouting for Uncle Abram to catch scary spiders and snakes.

There was no one asking questions about life in Iraq.

It was **very** quiet.

It was **too** quiet.

Abram sighed every time he found himself sitting in silence. He loved Lot like the son he had never had. Why had he let him move out? With half of the family fortunes? To the bad city?

Yes, life on Abram's campsite was worryingly quiet.

Every morning and every evening without fail, Abram would stand at the entrance of his tent with a tear in his eye and scan the dusty horizon in the hope that he would see his nephew coming home.

Weeks and months went by. Still Abram waited for Lot.

One morning, Abram was looking out for Lot as usual when he saw something most unusual racing up the hill towards the campsite.

It was a strange monstrous creature with crazed white eyes, flailing limbs and a terrible wheeze. It was covered in black squelchy goo and it stank. It stank like a million years' worth of rotting vegetables and decomposing sea creatures.

The monster lunged at Abram, but to his surprise it fell short, landing with a splat on Abram's feet. As a puddle of oil began to ooze out beneath it, Abram saw that it was not a monster after all, but a man.

'Sid? Is that you?' Abram gasped.

Now, Sid was from the valley of Siddim, which was right next door to the city of Sodom where Lot lived. That's how Abram knew Sid. Not a lot, but enough to recognise him even

when he was covered in sticky
black sludge.

'What on earth happened,
Sid?' Abram asked, pinching
his wrinkled old nose.

'The King of Sodom
started another fight,' Sid
spluttered, spitting out
mouthfuls of tar.

Globules of black sludge
splattered over Abram's tent.

'Not again!' Abram said, rolling his eyes. 'Someone needs to
teach that King to stop squabbling with his neighbours.'

'This time,' Sid groaned, 'he declared war on … King
Kerdor!'

Abram's jaw dropped. Everybody knew that you didn't pick
a fight with King Kerdor.

King Kerdor had the mightiest army in the whole land. It
wasn't just one mighty army – it was a whole bunch of mighty
armies all fighting together as one huge extra-mighty army.
What had the King of Sodom been thinking?

Sid's tears drew streaks on his blackened face. 'The King of Sodom just about escaped with his life, but nearly all his soldiers perished in the Black Swamps.'

You should never, ever go anywhere near the Black Swamps of Siddim. Especially at night. They are made up of pools of oil that seep up from deep underground. They smell so bad that birds fall out of the sky if they fly over them, rats run in the opposite direction and dogs that get too close howl in pain because the dreadful stench hurts their sensitive noses. Anyone unlucky enough to accidentally step into the Black Swamps is immediately sucked under, never to be seen again.

Abram suddenly felt breathless; and it wasn't because he'd been pinching his nose the entire time. He had a bad feeling that there was worse news to come.

'While I was trying to rescue the poor soldiers of Sodom,' Sid continued, 'King Kerdor's army ransacked Sodom. They stole everything.'

'Everything?' Abram asked.

'All their possessions. All their treasures. All their food supplies. Even all their people!'

'Everyone?'

Sid nodded sadly. 'Everyone. Including your nephew, Lot.'

If you have ever lost something, or someone, important to you, you might understand how Abram felt. Tears of grief poured down the old man's face as though they would never ever stop.

The other campsite residents began to gather at the old oak tree where Abram had slumped. Most of them didn't know what to say.

Some of them got the campfire going.

Others tried to help by making breakfast.

But a few of them stood around muttering. 'Serves the boy right! Lot should never have gone to Sodom in the first place. It was a bad choice. It is a bad city.'

Abram knew what they were saying was true. And this made him sadder than ever.

Meanwhile, with the help of a lot of soapy water and some tough scrubbing, Sid didn't look like a terrible bog monster any more. Good old clean Sid was back.

Abram watched the transformation and began to wonder if there might just be a way to get Lot back too.

'You'd **never** catch up with that marauding army now,' said Sid, blowing the last drops of tarry black oil out of his nostrils. 'It's impossible. You will **never** see your nephew again.'

'Never say never, Sid,' Abram said, getting to his feet. 'Nothing is impossible with God.'

A couple of days later and Sid was still trying to persuade Abram that his idea of rescuing Lot had zero chance of success. By then, they, and 317 men that Abram had paid to come too, had walked many miles on the trail of King Kerdor's army.

'Our feet are sore!' the men grumbled.

'Our sandwiches are stale!' they moaned.

'Our feet are so sore we put our stale sandwiches in our socks to cushion the blisters! AND NOW WE ARE STARVING!' they complained.

Everybody was ready to give up and go home when Abram suddenly spotted King Kerdor and his army of armies in the distance.

They edged closer. From the top of a wooded hill Abram could see the soldiers laughing and celebrating their victory. There were an awful lot of them.

'Right!' Abram announced. 'Operation Search-and-Find-a-Lot begins at midnight.'

'But Abram,' Sid piped up. 'Is Lot really worth the risk? We'll never get past that lot!'

'Never say never!' Abram said. But inside he was just as worried as Sid. Lot had made a terrible choice, and now 317 men plus Sid were risking their lives for him. But he loved Lot. And he trusted God. Abram would rescue his nephew – or die trying.

'On my first signal,' Abram said, 'you will creep silently down the hill.'

Everyone nodded.

'On my second signal you will split into groups and enter the camp from two directions at once.'

'Then what?' asked Sid.

'You'll see!' said Abram.

'You'll see?' grumbled the men. 'You'll see? In the middle of the night? We won't be able to see a thing. We'll be obliterated, pulverised, annihilated, done for.'

Everyone mumbled about this being the worst military plan ever in the history of bad military plans. But before they could think of an alternative, Abram gave the first signal.

And then he gave the second.

The reluctant men – all 318 of them – stormed King Kerdor's army camp with no idea what would happen next.

The desert creatures that had been enjoying a quiet night-
time picnic on the soldier's leftovers saw Abram's men arrive
and quickly scarpered – howling and squawking and hissing.
The soldiers' horses jumped in fright – neighing and tugging at
the carts laden with stolen goods from Sodom. The carts tipped
onto their sides and smashed into one another like crashing
dominos. All the stolen treasures clattered to the ground. That
woke up the lookout soldiers, who shouted warnings, but
they were far too late. Meanwhile, Abram's men were running
around in circles in a panic not quite knowing what to do next.

There wasn't
enough time for the
sleepy villains to organise
their own trousers, let alone
a defence strategy. Tripping over each other in the confusion,
they began running away down the road in fright, dragging
half-asleep prisoners with them.

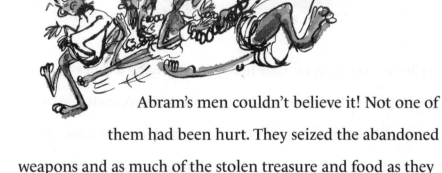

Abram's men couldn't believe it! Not one of
them had been hurt. They seized the abandoned
weapons and as much of the stolen treasure and food as they
could carry and began the chase.

They chased them up the road, across the hills, over the
river and across some more hills and still they couldn't catch
them.

Every time they got close, King Kerdor's army sped up a
little more.

Two miles later, Sid begged the old man to stop.

Two hundred miles later, Sid was still begging the old man to stop.

'Never!' Abram said.

'Never? What happened to **"never say never"?'** Sid looked round at the exhausted men behind him.

'I'm not going home without my nephew,' Abram said and picked up the pace.

The men were so tired their eyelids were drooping, their feet were dragging along through the dust and saliva was drooling down their chins. Occasionally one of them yawned, which made everyone else yawn. They were far too weary even to think about arguing with Abram. Nobody said a word.

Suddenly there was a noise in the leaves just ahead. Abram's old heart nearly missed a beat. Was this an ambush? Had he managed to chase King Kerdor's army for miles, only to be finished off by a bunch of robbers hiding in the undergrowth? His hopes of finding Lot faded away once more.

Abram's men were now scared as well as exhausted. They dropped their treasures and food supplies onto the ground. But just as they were about to turn to run for their lives, they heard something which didn't sound at all like a robber.

'Isn't that my grandmother's silver chamber pot?' asked a surprised voice from up a tree.

'I recognise that gold plate!' called another from the other side of the road.

'And I recognise something else!' said a third, jumping out in front of Abram. 'Look everyone! It's Sid!'

To Abram's great surprise, he soon found himself surrounded by people he recognised from Sodom. After being captured by King Kerdor, dragged away for hundreds of miles and then dumped in a forest to be eaten by wild animals, they couldn't thank Abram enough for rescuing them, and reuniting them with all their stolen treasures.

But where was Lot?

Eventually the old man spotted one prisoner standing at a distance, looking embarrassed and ashamed. He couldn't even look up as Abram ran over to him.

'I'm sorry, Uncle,' Lot mumbled. 'This is all my fault. If it weren't for my bad choices, you wouldn't have had to risk your

life – and everyone else's. I don't deserve to go home with you.'

Abram smiled as he put his arms around Lot and squeezed him tight. This was the boy he loved like the son he had never had. All was forgiven.

If you have ever lost and then found something, or someone, important to you, you might understand how Abram felt. Tears of happiness poured down the old man's face as he ran around telling everyone the great news.

'Let's celebrate!' Abram shouted at last. 'Lot who was lost has now been found!!'

Right there by the side of the road, one old but intrepid Iraqi man, his favourite nephew, all the freed captives, 317 men – and Sid – enjoyed a party the likes of which they would never see again.

'Never say never!' Abram smiled, tucking into a kebab.

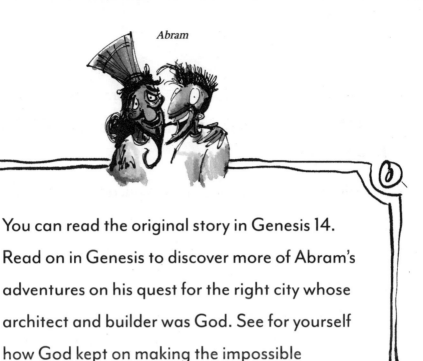

Abram

You can read the original story in Genesis 14.
Read on in Genesis to discover more of Abram's
adventures on his quest for the right city whose
architect and builder was God. See for yourself
how God kept on making the impossible
possible.

THE PRINCESS

THE TALE OF THE EXTRAORDINARY EGYPTIAN WHO CHOSE TO GO AGAINST THE FLOW

WELCOME TO EGYPT

Egypt is a country in Africa. Most of it is covered in desert, except for the lush green area around the Nile. The Nile is the longest river in the world and contains some of the world's largest reptiles – the Nile crocodiles. They won't hesitate to eat you if you get too close! Egypt also has lots of famous pyramids. These enormous stone tombs were once the home of the mummified bodies of the Pharaohs and their families and cats.

The Nile, the pyramids and the crocodiles that you can see in Egypt today would have looked just the same when the Bible started to get written. They would have shaped the life of the Egyptian hero in this tale. She was as inquisitive as a crocodile, as unshakeable as a pyramid and as unstoppable as the great river. She may have lived thousands of years ago, but one small thing she did changed the course of history forever.

Dads can be **so** annoying. Especially when your dad is the King. In particular when you are a princess and your dad is King Pharaoh, ruler of all ancient Egypt, who believes princesses shouldn't be allowed to do anything.

Here are some of the things King Pharaoh would say whenever he saw his daughter.

'**Don't** tidy up. **Don't** go to school. **Don't** open the door. **Don't** move. **Don't** speak. **Don't** think.'

The Princess had had enough of doing nothing. Sitting around looking important all day, every day, hour after hour: it was driving her crazy. She wanted to do something. Anything. But there she was stuck. She didn't know **what** to do.

She considered her problem as she sat in the library doing nothing one day. The walls around her were covered with writing. If only she could learn to read the hieroglyphs!

'Princesses don't read!' her father scoffed. 'Princesses don't write either! Princesses are supposed to **become** ancient history, not learn about it.'

Later, the Princess found herself sitting in the kitchen doing nothing again. She watched in awe as the chefs baked and boiled, flipped and fried, stewed and seasoned. How she would have loved to join them! But as soon as she opened her mouth to ask a question, it was filled with a spoonful of soup.

'Doesn't that taste good, Your Highness?' said the large chef who was cornering the Princess with his huge vat of bubbly brown mush. He smelled so strongly of garlic that she thought she might faint. Before she could answer, he popped a large chewy chunk of salted meat in the Princess's mouth. This was followed by one small fried fish, half a bread roll and a large handful of sticky dates.

The Princess's cheeks puffed out like a hamster. She tried to swallow all that food but couldn't. As soon as the chef pulled out a large boiled egg for her to try next, the whole lot erupted back in his face.

The next day the Princess sat in the courtroom – doing nothing. The King listened to people arriving with all their problems and the Princess began to feel she was quite good at doing this listening thing. But when her father passed judgment, she was shocked. It seemed it was not only princesses who couldn't do anything.

'Hebrews **don't** have days off,' Pharaoh said crossly, dismissing the poor man who had only asked for a couple of hours to help his neighbour fix his broken roof.

And so it continued: Hebrews **don't** go to school. Hebrews **don't** get paid. Hebrews **can't** have BABY BOYS.

The Princess went down to the river to do nothing there. Her two squabbling maids followed behind with enormous palm branches.

'It's my turn to fan her,' one of them said, pushing in front.

'That's not fair,' said the other. 'You had a turn yesterday. It's my turn.'

'Well, you don't do it properly.'

The first maid stuck out her tongue.

The second maid pretended not to notice.

'Well, I've got the biggest fan.'

'But I am her biggest fan.'

The Princess ignored them as usual and cast her attention elsewhere. On the opposite bank a young Hebrew girl was busy washing clothes in the hot sun, a baby strapped to her chest with a piece of cloth. Every so often the girl would look around nervously, before carrying on with her hard work scrubbing and rinsing.

The Princess wished that, just for a day, she could exchange her fan club and royal rules for bare feet, a huge pile of dirty washing and a sense of purpose and achievement.

It wasn't long before the riverbank girl was joined by some Hebrew friends, busy with chores of their own. As they all chatted together, they had no idea that the Princess, who was pretending to be asleep on the opposite bank, was listening to every word they said.

'My back aches,' said one as she washed, peeled and chopped vegetables in the shallows.

'Aching back? At least you haven't got sore knuckles,' moaned another, scrubbing at a very dirty pan.

A third girl, standing waist deep in the river, threw her hands up in the air. 'You think you've got life hard with sore knuckles? I've twisted my ankle – do you know how hard it is to carry water **and** hop?'

The Princess tried hard not to laugh. She didn't want the girls to guess she could hear them.

'You think that's tough?' said the girl carrying the baby. 'Try cooking dinner with one hand while changing your brother's nappy with the other!'

The other girls screwed up their faces. 'Eeuuurgh!'

'I bet it doesn't smell as terrible as Pharaoh's bad breath ...' one of them joked, before they all joined in the punchline: 'It sphinx!'

Their giggles died away and they carried on working. The next voice the Princess heard was that of the first riverbank girl – and she wasn't joking at all.

'That evil maniac Pharaoh is working our parents to death. I hardly see mine any more. Each day I have to take care of my brothers for longer and longer. And I have to do more and more chores. If only things could go back to how they were.'

'Meanwhile,' her friend added, glancing across the river and lowering her voice, 'Princess Fancy-Pants Lazybones McSmugface over there never even lifts a finger! She just sleeps all day. It's so unfair!'

'I wish I could swap places with her. Just for a day,' the riverbank girl sighed.

One of her friend's put an arm around her shoulder. 'Don't worry, Miriam. Keep praying. God will save us all soon.'

The Princess didn't know who this God was, but now she had a name – Miriam – for the riverbank girl with the baby. She also had a new name for herself: Princess Fancy-Pants Lazybones McSmugface! If only she could tell the girls how she really felt. Swish clothes didn't make her happy. She wasn't being lazy by choice. She would gladly lift all of her fingers to help. She just didn't know how.

'Quick, let's go before the palace guard catches us,' the

Princess heard one of the girls say suddenly. 'We don't want him throwing your baby into the river.'

Miriam had already grabbed her washing piles and was clutching them to her chest to shield her tiny brother.

'It's not fair that Pharaoh is murdering our baby boys,' she cried.

'My mum calls him a **big bully** with a **big belly**,' said her friend, placing her large pitcher of water on her head. 'But my dad says he's mean because he is scared of all the mummies in Egypt!'

With that, the girls vanished into the reeds just moments before the palace guard appeared.

The Princess was shocked. Surely Pharaoh wouldn't have taken Miriam's baby away. Surely her dad couldn't be so cruel. How could anyone want to harm an innocent baby?

The Princess did not have to wait long to have her worst fears confirmed. That evening, just before dinner, Pharaoh's angry voice was heard reverberating around the courtyards of the palace.

'Eight?'

'Er, yessir,' replied the palace guard.

'Eight more boys?' Pharaoh's voice was getting louder.

The guard's voice, however, was getting quieter. 'Yessir.'

The Princess peeped out of the window. She could see her father's face growing redder with each word.

'I SAID NO MORE BABY BOYS! I will not let my country be overrun by worthless Hebrew slaves! No! No! NO!!!!'

'Yessir,' whispered the palace guard, cowering. But Pharaoh still hadn't finished.

'GO! Annihilate them! In the Nile! All eight to be fed to the crocodiles! And make it snappy!'

That night, the Princess tossed and turned. How could her own father be such a monster! She imagined him seizing Miriam and her baby and hurling them both into the river. In her nightmares they were being carried away on the current,

faster and faster, further and further. They called for help as they sank beneath the murky water, circled by enormous hungry crocodiles. The Princess watched, frozen. She couldn't lift even a finger.

As soon as the sun's first rays lit the horizon, the Princess went down to the river. Several Hebrew girls were already sitting in silence trying to catch small fish for their breakfast.

There was one empty spot on the riverbank. Miriam and her baby brother were missing!

The Princess felt terrible. She should have done something while she could. But she wasn't used to **doing** things. She wasn't **allowed** to do things. She didn't even know **how** to do things. And now … it was too late.

Nobody could see her tears as she swam up and down. The Princess cried for all the babies who had died. For all the sisters and brothers and mothers and fathers who had suffered. For all the terrible things her own father was doing to the Hebrew people. She cried for herself and her own uselessness.

Just then she heard a noise. Was it her own voice? Had she cried out loud?

The Princess swam a bit further before hearing the noise again – it sounded suspiciously like … a baby. But how could there be a baby in the middle of the river? Perhaps it was the ghosts of all the dead babies haunting her because she hadn't done anything to help them.

The Princess began to make her way towards the reed bed where the crying sounds seemed to have come from. She was trying hard to listen but all she could hear was the sound of her two maids arguing on the bank.

'What is she doing? She knows princesses aren't allowed to do anything.'

'Stop her!'

'No, you stop her.'

'No, you.'

'Stop pushing me.'

With that, the Princess heard a loud splash, and a few minutes later, one of the maids, looking very sorry for herself, had appeared beside her in the reed bed in the middle of the river.

'Let me get that, Your Highness!' the maid said, her hair full of river weeds. 'It looks like those Hebrew women have been throwing their shopping bags in the river again. It's a disgrace. Terribly bad for the environment.'

'Hang on!' said the Princess. She wanted to take a look inside the basket that the maid had managed to pull out of the reeds.

'No, you hang on to me, milady,' said the maid, misunderstanding the Princess. 'I'll get you and this pile of rubbish safely back to shore while that other maid stands there being useless.'

The Princess suddenly leapt into action in a most unprincess-like way.

she tackled the maid, grabbed the basket,

fought her way out of the reeds, battled the current,

karate kicked a crocodile (or was it just a log?)

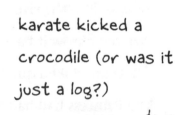

and clambered up the slippery, muddy bank with a whoop.

Then, finding a place in the
shade, she carefully set the basket
down on the grass. Slowly she
parted the folds of the dry sheet
inside.

'Eeuugh! Yuk!' The two
maids beside her turned their noses up in disgust.

'It looks like a drowned rat,' said one.

'It smells like a drowned rat too,' said the other.

This was the first thing the Princess had ever heard them
agree on. But their partnership didn't last long.

'It's a stinky Hebrew baby!' said the first maid. 'Quick!
Throw it back in the river.'

'No, you throw it back in the river.'

'You do it! And quick, before Pharaoh finds out.'

The Princess had had enough. 'Pharaoh must not find
out!' she snapped. 'I will deal with this myself. And if either of
you breathe a word to anyone, I will personally lock you in a
pyramid for a thousand years.'

The two maids quickly scuttled away in panic, leaving the
Princess alone with the baby she had pulled out of the river.

The Princess looked at him squinting in the sunlight. She stroked his soft skin and watched his chest rising and falling gently with each breath. She carefully lifted him and let him nestle against her. How could anyone want to hurt such a beautiful boy?

Just then the Princess noticed a slight movement in the bulrushes. A pair of scared eyes were watching her. A pair of eyes that seemed strangely familiar.

'Miriam? Miriam! You're alive! What are you doing here – on the wrong side of the river? My father will kill you if he sees you! You shouldn't be risking your life like this.'

Miriam didn't have time to ask how the Princess knew her name, or why she hadn't thrown the boy straight back in the river. The words tumbled out of her. 'My brother ... My mum put him in the basket ... To get him away from Pharaoh ... He was supposed to go further downstream ... She believed God would save him, but ...'

This God again. Saving people again. The Princess quite liked the sound of him. He was certainly nothing like Pharaoh. She looked Miriam in the eye.

'Tell your mother I saved him from the river. Now I have to save him from my father. But don't worry – I will do everything I can for him.'

The Princess laid the baby in Miriam's arms.

'Take him, please, while I persuade Pharaoh. And take my royal golden bangle too. Now no palace guard will dare touch either of you.'

The Princess watched as Miriam disappeared with the baby she had rescued. Or had the baby rescued her? He had made her feel alive. He had given her life purpose. Now, finally, she knew exactly what she was going to do.

Later that evening, the princess sat next to her father at dinner time and waited for him to finish his soup.

'Please could I adopt a Hebrew boy I pulled out of the river?'

'**ABSOLUTELY NOT,**' bellowed Pharaoh angrily.

The next day at dinner she tried again.

'Please let me adopt the Hebrew boy.'

'**I SAID NO!**'

Every evening she asked the same question.

'Please let me adopt the Hebrew boy.'

'NO! And don't ask again.'

'Please let me adopt the Hebrew boy.'

'NOOOOOO!!!!'

'Please let me adopt the Hebrew boy.'

'NO.'

'Can I adopt the Hebrew boy?'

'NO! Egyptian Princesses DO NOT adopt HEBREW BOYS.'

Five months, three weeks and six days later, Pharaoh couldn't take it any longer.

'Fine! OK then! Adopt the boy! Just LEAVE ME ALONE!'

Daughters, it turned out, can be **SO** annoying.

The Princess smiled. She had done it! She had done something when everyone told her she couldn't do anything. She had made a difference. A little, tiny difference to one little, tiny child.

Little did she know that something **big** was about to happen. That tiny child she had saved would, one day, in turn, with God's help, save an entire nation. A million Hebrew prayers would be answered because one Egyptian Princess had done something extraordinary.

You can read the Bible's account of the
Princess, Miriam and the baby, who they
named Moses, in Exodus 2. In the rest of
Exodus you will find out how Moses annoyed
Pharaoh and how God used him to save all
the Hebrew slaves.

RUTH

THE TALE OF THE GIANT-HEARTED JORDANIAN WHO WENT THE EXTRA MILE

WELCOME TO JORDAN

Many years ago, a plane accidentally crashed into a refugee camp in the small country of Jordan killing many people. A baby was pulled out of the rubble, but the rescuers gave her up for dead. However, several hours later someone saw that she was still breathing and rushed her to the hospital. It just so happened that the Queen of Jordan was at the same hospital at the same time for a dental appointment. When the Queen of Jordan saw the little girl, she fell in love with her. She helped look after her until

she was healthy again and adopted her into the Jordanian Royal Family.

This true story echoes another incredible act of kindness from thousands of years earlier when Jordan was known as Moab. It starts with another refugee living in Jordan. Her family was wiped out too. Her life seemed to be over. But it wasn't. Someone very special was about to come into her life and together they would both end up being included in a royal family unlike any other.

R uth and Orpah were hiding in some prickly bushes and staring at a small tumbledown cottage. The two girls knew all about the rumours going around. The stories of an old woman who had moved in and had been seen muttering spells under her breath. The reports of banging and sawing and digging. The claims that children had been heard crying and moaning in the middle of the night. It was all very spooky, very strange and very, very suspicious.

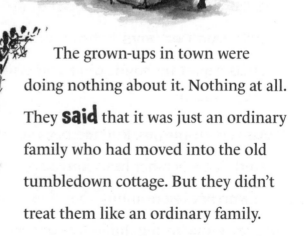

The grown-ups in town were doing nothing about it. Nothing at all. They **said** that it was just an ordinary family who had moved into the old tumbledown cottage. But they didn't treat them like an ordinary family.

They ignored them. They avoided them. And that made it **even more suspicious.**

That's why Ruth and Orpah had decided **they** would do something. **They** would investigate. **They** would reveal the shocking truth. **They** would go down in history for saving the world from whatever evil force had moved into their neighbourhood.

Their career as personal investigators had not got off to a good start. Hiding in those prickly bushes opposite the tumbledown cottage, the cramped surveillance team had only noted the following:

8.01 a.m. Family eating breakfast.

8.05 a.m. Two boys waving to man leaving house.

8:10 a.m. Two boys helping woman wash dishes.

8:20 a.m. Two boys playing in garden.

'This is very suspicious, Ruth,' Orpah said with a shiver.

Ruth scratched her head. She was beginning to feel hungry, and the prickles were annoying her. 'But Orpah, aren't they just doing the same boring things we do every day?'

Orpah nodded. 'That's what makes it SOOOO suspicious.'

'Ah, I see!' Ruth said. 'Wait! I don't see!'

'Me neither. Let's move closer – to get a better view.'

The two girls pushed and pulled each other up into the branches of a large, leafy tree that overhung the strangers' garden.

It was a great vantage point. Ruth and Orpah could see that among the weeds a vegetable patch had been dug carefully and things were beginning to grow in neat lines. Inside the house, which was small and bare, a woman was working hard. Two boys squatted at her feet, swatting flies and lizards. Now the girls could make the observations they had been hoping for:

One pair of worn red slippers (creepy)

Two sardine sandwiches (fishy)

Half a bar of soap (slippery)

One small sock (odd)

Ruth and Orpah were so busy observing that they failed to observe a very large crack on the branch they were sitting on.

One minute they were letting their imaginations run wild, the next their bodies were tumbling head over heels towards the hard, dry ground.

'Ouch!' cried Orpah, pulling a large thorn out of her leg. She had landed upside down in a pile of weeds, which stung her skin. Escaping from the brambles, she hobbled away as fast as she could, leaving her friend lying unconscious on a row of radishes.

When Ruth woke up she was inside the gloomy house. Pain shot up and down her arm, making her wince. As the room came into focus, she saw three pairs of wide eyes looking right back at her. Her instinct was to run. But her body wouldn't move.

'Kilion! She's waking up!' one of the boys whispered, his eyes lighting up with relief.

'Are you sure she doesn't bite, Mahlon?' said the other boy. He edged a little closer to his older brother. 'You said we couldn't trust the Moa**bites** from **Jaw**-dan.'

'Moabites from Jordan don't really bite, silly.' The older boy laughed and pretended to gnaw at his brother's shoulder. 'At least, I hope they don't.'

He turned to Ruth. 'Well? Do you?'

Ruth couldn't answer because just at that moment the boy's mother began tipping a sweet, warm liquid into her mouth. Perhaps it was a potion that would turn her into a lizard.

Her eyes opened wide in panic.

That made Mahlon laugh. He pulled a face too.

That made Kilion laugh.

Ruth, having checked she was not a lizard, smiled back. Soon, they were all giggling uncontrollably, and she had forgotten all about her sore arm and bump on the head.

As Ruth walked home later that evening, she couldn't stop thinking about the family in the tumbledown cottage. They were nothing like she had imagined them to be. The boys were so funny. Especially Mahlon. Ruth pulled out her page of observations and crossed each one out. She had learned some new things she wanted to remember:

1. Don't spy on your neighbours: you might jump to conclusions and hurt yourself and others.
2. It is not nice for a so-called best friend to ditch you in your hour of need.
3. Sometimes strange people are much kinder than you think.
4. Good things can happen when you least expect them.
5. It is possible to fall out of a tree and fall in love at the same time.

The next day, Ruth took flowers to apologise for causing such trouble and ended up staying for tea. She learned that the boys' mother was called Naomi, their father was called Elimelek and between them they rustled up the most delicious bread.

The next day, Ruth took a card to say thank you for tea and ended up staying for dinner. She discovered that if Mahlon's family hadn't escaped to Jordan, they would have starved to death in a place called Bethlehem. She couldn't wait to tell Orpah the dramatic tale of the refugee family on the run. Perhaps she did have a career as an investigator after all.

The next day, Orpah joined Ruth as she delivered a 'thank you for dinner' plate of biscuits and ended up spending the whole weekend there. On Saturday morning, they joined in the family's tradition of pancakes and prayers.

Soon, every Saturday morning was spent with Mahlon's family. Then every Saturday afternoon. And shortly after, Sundays, evenings and holidays too.

Nobody was surprised when, a few years later, Ruth married Mahlon and Orpah married Kilion and the four of them, together with Naomi and Elimelek, lived happily ever after in the old tumbledown cottage in Jordan.

Except they didn't. This story is based on a true story and in most true stories people tend to live **happily-for-a-while** until an **unhappily-for-a-while** takes over. Poor Ruth was about to experience three terribly unhappy events.

Unhappy event 1: Elimelek died. Everyone cried, the neighbours visited to pay their respects and Mahlon and Kilion had to work harder to pay the bills.

Unhappy event 2: Mahlon and Kilion got sick and died. Everyone cried some more. The neighbours stayed away. Perhaps tragedy was contagious.

Unhappy event 3: Naomi made an announcement. With no husband, no sons, no money, no friends and no hope, life in Jordan was just too hard. She was heading back to Bethlehem.

Ruth was worried. What if Naomi couldn't manage such a long and dangerous journey? What if they all got to Bethlehem and Naomi's friends had gone? What if her old house had holes in the roof or animals had moved in? Where would they all live?

Naomi was worried too. What if Ruth and Orpah hated Bethlehem? What if they got treated badly? What if she died and they had to come back to Jordan by themselves?

Naomi made another announcement. She would go alone.

'Phew!' burst Orpah, giving the old lady a quick hug. 'With all due respect, living with a miserable old woman with no money in a faraway country where I couldn't speak the language would be no fun at all.'

Ruth and Naomi watched Orpah skip away down the road. Naomi turned sadly to Ruth and opened her arms wide.

'Goodbye Ruth. Go home to your parents too.'

Ruth shook her head. She would not abandon Naomi in her hour of need.

'I will go wherever you go,' Ruth said.

Naomi took a deep breath. Pointing her finger in Ruth's face, she raised her voice. 'You, young lady, will stay right here.'

'I will stay wherever you stay,' Ruth said firmly.

'But I'm going to stay in faraway Bethlehem,' Naomi insisted, 'where I will die.'

Ruth didn't falter. 'I will die wherever you die,' she said. 'I'll even be buried wherever you're buried.'

'In a Jewish graveyard?' Naomi was shocked. It was the last place a normal Moabite woman from Jordan would have wanted to end up.

'Your God is my God now,' Ruth said solemnly. She had seen something special in the way Mahlon's family had trusted God, despite all that had happened to them.

'Your God brought us together – he is the only one who can tear us apart,' she continued.

With that, Ruth picked up the bags in one arm, slipped her other arm under Naomi's and argued with her all the way to the border. And beyond.

A few weeks, and many, many miles later, children were seen whispering. There were suspicious smells coming from Bethlehem's abandoned tumbledown cottage. They'd heard scary noises. They'd seen strange people.

Ruth ignored the children whispering. She ignored the women who ignored her or looked down their noses at her. She ignored the men who spat in her face. But she couldn't ignore Naomi growing weaker and weaker. They had run out of food. Ruth had to do something. Something desperate. Something dangerous.

That's why she found herself foraging for grain in a wheat field called Rock Bottom.

Nobody but the birds and the poorest of the poor ever went to Rock Bottom. It lay on the edge of the wrong side of town, and although it was the only place you were allowed to help yourself to leftover grain, most people were far too scared

of the hot sun, the wild creatures,
the sharp rocks, or even worse,
the rough, heartless farmers who
harvested there.

'Hey!'

Ruth dropped her grains
in fright. The few Rock Bottom
grains that had taken her hours
to collect. The grains that could be
ground into flour to make a tiny
roll that would mean the difference
between life and death for Naomi. A
harvester was headed straight for her.
So much for the bread she
was hoping to make. Now
she was toast.

'I've heard about you,' the man
called. 'About you and Naomi.'

Ruth braced herself for the usual insults. 'You don't belong
here. Refugees don't deserve help. Go back to where you came
from – and take that old witch with you.'

But in that moment on that day on the edge of Rock Bottom, something snapped inside of Ruth. She glued her hands to her hips and looked the man in the eye.

'Do what you like to me, but don't say anything bad about Naomi. She may be grumpy, but she is old, she's lost everything and she doesn't deserve to end her days hungry and lonely.'

'I see,' said the man, now standing within kicking distance.

'Good.' Ruth swallowed. 'Wait. You see? What do you see?'

'I see …' he said slowly, 'I see a girl who has no grain, but a lot of grit. I see a young woman who left everything behind – country, family and friends – to take care of a penniless old Jewish woman. I see a great sacrifice. I see a giant kindness.'

'Well, Mr …' Ruth didn't quite know what to say next.

'Boaz. Call me Boaz.'

'Boaz?' Ruth repeated, looking at him sideways. 'As in ... Mr Boaz ... who ... who owns the land?'

The man nodded and left. Ruth couldn't believe she had been so rude – to one of the most important men in town. What would Naomi say?!

Ruth replayed the conversation over and over in her head. For the rest of the day, for some strange reason, none of the harvesters insulted her, not even once, and she just kept finding whole handfuls of wheat in her path. It was all rather ... suspicious.

So Ruth and Naomi didn't go hungry after all. Quite the opposite! After a few more dates at Rock Bottom, Boaz and Ruth fell in love. They got married with Naomi's blessing, had a baby boy, became much-loved celebrities in the town and everyone lived happily ever after. The end.

Except it wasn't the end.

Because this, like many Bible stories, is a story that goes on, and on, and gets better and better.

Years later, a boy called David was born into Ruth's family. He became famous for fighting giants, writing poetry, being kind to a boy everyone else had forgotten about – and becoming King.

And many years after that, another boy was born into Ruth's family. He was born in a stable not far from where Ruth had lived. His name was Jesus. He was the kindest person who has ever lived. He is God himself, the King of Kings.

Many, many, years after that, you and I were born into a world where there are millions of people like Naomi: those who have lost friends and family and homes and country. Ruth's story continues in all of us who offer them kindness, friendship and hope in Jesus' name.

Ruth went down in history for being kind to an old refugee lady. She even got a whole book of the Bible named after her. Read it for yourself sometime, and be inspired to go the extra mile for someone who needs it.

NAAMAN

THE TALE OF THE SYRIAN SUPERVILLAIN WHO HAD A DANGEROUS SECRET

WELCOME TO SYRIA

Syria was once a beautiful country with historic castles,
fast trains, swanky hotels and seaside resorts. Fresh bread
and cakes were baked on the corners of streets. Famous
storytellers performed to audiences from far and wide, as
onlookers enjoyed ice-cream in the town squares.

Unfortunately, there was a terrible war in Syria that
has buried those wonderful things under piles of rubble.
One day, perhaps, they will rise from the ashes and Syria

will be beautiful, peaceful and safe once more.

In Bible times, like today, the Syrian army was often in the news – and not for good reasons. It was the last place on earth you would expect to hear the story of a powerful villain doing something great.

But the Bible is full of surprises – and it fills us with hope that God can change even the things that are most terrifying and terrible.

So, what are you good at? Perhaps you don't think you are good at anything, but everyone is born to shine at something. Some people are great at sports, others are amazing at music or maths or memorising things. You might know someone who is brilliant at making people smile, or who can swim a whole length underwater or who comes up with inventive ideas to help their neighbours. Washing the car, growing wonky carrots, cleaning under the bed, turning somersaults, getting out of trouble: there are just so many good things to be good at.

Unfortunately for the world, General Naaman's skill set seemed to involve being terribly good at killing people. He brought death and destruction wherever he went. He was so good at it, the King of Syria put the bloodthirsty supervillain in charge of his entire army.

Naaman trained his army to kill people in all sorts of ways.

swords

stoning

Spears

Wild dogs

Deep pits

Poison

catapults

Bow and arrow

Drowning

Fire

You name it –
Naaman was the expert
in it. Oh yes, he was
very, very good at
killing people.

While everyone is born to shine, we all have weaknesses
too. Me. You. Parents. Friends. Carers. Teachers. Even
supervillains in the Syrian army. Like many people, General
Naaman didn't like to talk about his problems. And there was
one particular problem he hadn't mentioned to anyone at all –
not even his wife.

'Naaman, my dear,' she said one day, waltzing into the
room in her latest designer outfit, 'what is it with those gloves?
You wear them at breakfast. You wear them when you brush
your teeth. You wear them when you swim. You even wear
them to bed!'

'I love these gloves.' Naaman lied, avoiding his wife's glare. 'They are my favourite. Don't you think they make me look important? And handsome?'

You see, underneath his gloves, Naaman's hands were covered in white patches. They didn't hurt, but they looked

horrible, there was no cure, and eventually they would kill him.

Naaman had seen others suffer with the same disease. He had kicked them out of the army, fired them from working in his house, and sneered at them as they lay rotting like rubbish in ditches by the side of the road. Now it seemed like it was about to be his turn to rot in a ditch.

General Naaman may have been invincible on the battlefield, but he couldn't win a fight against the invisible nerve-destroying disease. Every time he looked at his skin, he felt sick with worry.

'Naaman, my dear,' his wife said one morning, tucking into

a huge pile of scrambled eggs, 'what's wrong with the food on your plate?' You hardly touch your breakfast. You skip lunch. You leave your dinner to go cold and then throw half of it away. What's eating you?'

'I'm just not hungry.' Naaman lied again, tightening the belt on his tunic. 'I'm on a diet. I'm too busy planning how to kill people. I'm bored of the same food day after day.'

One evening Naaman came home from work and slumped down in his favourite chair. Checking to make sure his wife was out, and that nobody was looking, he took off his gloves just for a second to bite his nails. The butler, who was inspecting the garden, happened to glance through the window at that exact second and saw Naaman's diseased hands.

The **butler** told the **laundry lady** who told the **chef** who told the **chariot driver** who told a **young housemaid**.

'So that's why he's been so grumpy recently,' said the butler.

'That's why he won't ever take off those gloves,' said the laundry lady.

'That's why he's been off his food,' said the chef.

'He's scared,' said the chariot driver.

'And he's dying,' said
the housemaid.

'Do we feel sorry for him?'
asked the laundry lady.

'No, we don't!' said the
butler and the chef and the
chariot driver.

'Well, I feel a little bit
sorry for him,' admitted the
young housemaid.

The chariot driver and
the gardener and the butler
and the chef stared at the young housemaid in disbelief. They
couldn't believe their ears. Nobody had ever felt sorry for
Naaman, nobody at all.

Naaman treated everyone like dirt. And he treated his
servants worse than dirt. But he treated the young housemaid
even worse than that.

Perhaps it was because she wasn't Syrian. Perhaps it was
because she was from another country called Samaria. Or
maybe it was because he had paid so little for her when he

had bought her at the slave market as a present for his wife. Whatever the reason, he certainly didn't care one bit that this young girl had been kidnapped and smuggled out of her country. He didn't give half a hoot that she'd lost her home and family. He shouted at her and scolded her and made her life even more miserable than it already was.

I don't know about you, but if I had been kidnapped and forced to work for one of the scariest men in Syria, I would be pretty mad. So mad, in fact, that I might be secretly pleased if my cruel, bloodthirsty boss got a terrible skin disease. Finally he would understand what it was like to lose his home and family and be treated like dirt. It would totally serve him right.

Despite her hard and unhappy life, the young Samaritan housemaid was good at one really important thing – and that was following God. That was why she decided to do what she could to help her boss.

'Are you crazy?' said the chef.

'You did what?!' said the laundry lady.

'You could have been executed!' said the butler.

'Or worse!' said the chariot driver, remembering all the ways Naaman liked to finish people off.

You see, that morning the young
housemaid had plucked up the courage
to speak to Naaman's wife as
she was pinning her hair
into the latest style. The
housemaid had told her
about Naaman's skin
condition and explained
that she had been
praying for him.

She had even dared
tell her mistress about a
well-known prophet, back
in Israel, who could cure
Naaman's deadly disease.

'Naaman, my dear,'
his wife said later as she
settled onto her sun
lounger. 'What is it with
keeping secrets? Were you
too scared to tell me about

a silly rash? Is this problem too difficult for you to fix? Are you too lazy to go and see the prophet in Israel who has the cure?'

By the end of that day, Naaman, with a troop of soldiers and a handful of servants, found himself on his way to Samaria. As he bumped along the road in his chariot he began to wonder. How had his wife found out about his terrible skin disease? How had she heard about this so-called prophet? And what on earth was he doing travelling to Israel, not to attack it as he usually did, but in search of a cure he was pretty sure did not exist?

A few days later Naaman's arrival was announced at the royal palace with a fanfare. His chariots and horses and soldiers filled the courtyard while he himself was ushered to the banquet room to wait for the King. Upstairs, the royal advisor tried to persuade the King to greet his grim guest.

'Excuse me, Your Royal Highness. General Naaman is here!'

'What?!' The King jumped out of his enormous bed in fright. 'The Assassin from Aleppo? The Malicious Murderer? THE SADISTIC SUPERVILLAIN?'

'Yes. Although he said we should just call him Naaman.'

'Err… did you try telling him we were out?' asked the King shivering in his pyjamas.

The royal advisor shuffled uncomfortably. 'He says he wants you to give him the cure for his skin disease. And…' he

added quickly, 'he's brought gifts for you.'

'It must be a trick. I don't trust him one little bit,' whimpered the King, hiding in the

pile of dust under his bed and chewing his pyjama sleeve.

The news of the stand-off spread around the whole country. Naaman got angrier and angrier waiting for the King to hand over the cure, and the King refused to come out from under his bed until Naaman had gone. Everyone knew there was no cure. But nobody dared tell the General.

Just when Naaman was about to declare war on Israel for being unbearably rude to an important Syrian General, the royal advisor rushed in with a note that arrived.

'Naaman: Go to the prophet Elisha's house in Gilgal in Samaria.'

You might have thought that Naaman would have been grateful. But Naaman was not grateful at all – he was furious.

'I am furious!' Naaman told his servants. **'First** the King refused to see me. **Then,** instead of telling the prophet to meet me at the palace, I am being sent to the back of beyond to try and find him. **Don't** these people have any idea who I am? **Don't** they realise I could obliterate their country and turn it into a **pile of rubble?'**

Now, a VIP welcome at Elisha's house might have helped Naaman calm down. But there was no VIP welcome. Not even a whiff of one. There was no lavish banquet, no live music, not even a single flag waving. All Naaman found when he arrived in Gilgal was yet another annoying note.

Elisha
(prophet of God)

'Naaman: Go to the River Jordan. Bathe seven times.'

'That's it!' Naaman said, stamping

his feet in anger. 'I've never been so insulted in all my

life. Who do these people think they are ordering me around?

Whatever will they tell me

to do next? Climb their

mountain? Plough their

fields? Sweep their

streets. Well I'm not going to bathe in their filthy river. I am going straight back to Syria. I've got an invasion to organise.'

'I'm scared,' said the laundry lady, as Naaman climbed into the chariot spitting and scowling.

'**He's gonna take this out on us,**' said the butler, quivering.

'**This can't end well,**' said the chef, shaking his head sadly.

'**Do we feel sorry for him?**' asked the chariot driver.

'**No, we don't!**'

'Well, I feel a little bit sorry for him,' whispered the young housemaid.

The other servants looked on in shock and horror as the young Samaritan housemaid proceeded to walk straight up to her spitting and scowling boss. She looked him right in the eye and opened her mouth to speak.

'Excuse me, General,' she said, feeling a lot more nervous than she looked, 'Do you… should you… maybe… since we've come all this way … don't you even want to try… with the bathing seven times in the River Jordan?

'You've nothing to lose as it's on our

way home, and it won't cost a penny. Surely, you're

not too proud to try?'

For a moment Naaman thought the whole world had gone

crazy. Why was everyone being so rude to him today? First the

King, then the prophet and now this housemaid! He was far

more powerful than any of them. He would show them. He

would bathe in the river and prove to the world that he was

right and they were wrong. Then he would have all the reasons he needed to destroy the country and everyone in it.

Naaman's nerves were so damaged that he couldn't feel the coldness of the water or the sharpness of the stones on his feet. When he was as deep as he could get, he washed himself all over from head to toe with the muddy water. Suddenly, with his uniform lying limp on the bank, and with his scabby, scaly, sore skin on show for all to see, he began to feel very unimportant.

What if the King was right? Perhaps he wasn't worth getting out of bed for, after all. What if the prophet was right? Why should he expect VIP treatment after the way he'd treated others? What if the housemaid was right? Perhaps he was just too proud. He didn't deserve to be cured at all.

Naaman looked at his horrible, diseased skin and realised he was just as horrible and diseased on the inside. He washed again and again – seven times altogether. With each dip he noticed more people on the riverbanks pointing and laughing. He felt as foolish as he looked. He hung his head in shame and started to pray.

'I am a terrible person. I've killed people. I've threatened people. I've enslaved people. I treat everyone as though they were less important than me. I've been selfish and proud and mean. I'm sorry for all that now. If anyone deserves this death sentence, it's me.'

'Find a towel!' said the butler.

'Help him up the bank!' said the chariot driver.

'Grab his hand!' said the chef.

'I'm not touching his mouldy hand!' said the laundry lady. She screwed up her face in disgust at the very thought.

'**Look!**' said the young housemaid, pointing excitedly at Naaman. '**It's a miracle!**'

Naaman's servants rushed forward. As Naaman lifted his hands up, he saw his skin: smooth, brown and beautiful. There wasn't a trace of white anywhere on his whole body. Tears poured down his face as he stood dripping on the bank. He was free!

All the way back to Elisha's house, Naaman couldn't stop looking at his hands and his feet. He could hardly believe it! But he wasn't just different on the outside: inside he had changed too. He had spent his whole life being really good at being really bad. For the rest of his life he wanted to learn how to be really good at following the God who had saved him.

This time Elisha opened the door wide and welcomed Naaman in. They talked for hours. Naaman wanted to know everything about Israel's God, and how he could honour him, even in his difficult position as the General of the Syrian Army.

Three years later, the King of Syria was pacing up and down in his chamber. 'I don't believe it!' he shouted angrily. 'Every time we launch an attack at Israel, they know exactly where we will be. They are ready and waiting for us. Our mighty army is being humiliated time and again by this tiny little excuse for a nation. How are they making us look so stupid? Someone is leaking intelligence.

'Yes, my King, of course,' replied Naaman calmly.

General Naaman left the King's palace, smiling to himself and thanking the God of Israel that the latest round of border raids had led to no casualties, and no new slaves. War had been averted again. Israel was safe.

Since Elisha had sent him back to Syria, Naaman had a new secret. This one turned out to be even more dangerous than a terrible skin disease. Every day he risked his life fighting for peace.

For now, all he had to do was pretend to look for a spy, and his secret, as well as his new friends in Israel, would be safe for a bit longer.

You can read this story of the supervillain-turned-international-peacemaker for yourself in 2 Kings 5 and 6. These historic books of the Bible show us the amazing things God can do with the least likely people who bravely choose to follow him.

ESTHER

THE TALE OF THE IMPORTANT IRANIAN WHO WISHED HER LIFE AWAY

WELCOME TO IRAN

If you are ever lucky enough to go to Iran, you will discover
that the Iranian people are very hospitable. You will
probably get invited into lots of homes and to lots of
parties, where they will love talking to you about their
family and their favourite sports like football and wrestling.
They will most certainly offer you lots of delicious-looking
food. Often it is served to you while you sit on beautiful
Persian rugs like an enormous indoor picnic. The polite
thing to do is to refuse first of all, but, don't worry, you will
get to try everything in the end. If you are really lucky, there

might be cookies at the end of the meal as cookies, believe it or not, were invented in Iran.

This story from the Bible is set in one of the oldest cities in the world. It is the ancient citadel of Susa, which is now called Shush, and can be found in modern-day Iran. In Bible times, Iran was part of a huge empire which stretched from India to Egypt to Greece. The story may not involve cookies but look out for all the parties. Being hospitable can make a really big difference, especially when trouble is brewing.

Do you ever wish you lived in a bigger house, or had fancier clothes, or mountains of money? Do you sometimes dream about winning competitions, hanging out with famous people or hosting huge parties? Or perhaps you are more the sort of person who imagines an exciting career in campaigning for world peace?

Most people believe their life would be perfect if only their wishes were to come true. Most people have no such luck. But what if they did get what they wished for? And what if it all turned out to be terribly dreadful?

Poor Esther was sitting in her bedroom wishing she were somewhere else. The room was cold and dusty, and she was hungry and fed up. Her overprotective Uncle Mordecai had told her she couldn't stay out late with her friends. Again.

'I have to keep you safe, Esther,' he
had said. 'It's only because I love you.
The world can be a dangerous place.
Especially for **people like us.'**

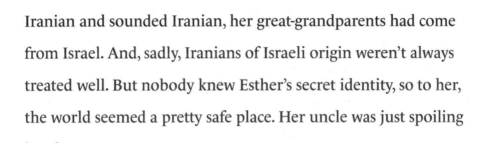

Esther, you see, had a secret she
hadn't told anyone. Although she looked
Iranian and sounded Iranian, her great-grandparents had come
from Israel. And, sadly, Iranians of Israeli origin weren't always
treated well. But nobody knew Esther's secret identity, so to her,
the world seemed a pretty safe place. Her uncle was just spoiling
her fun.

When Esther met her friends in town
the next day, they were all laughing about
their late-night antics. Esther felt left out.
And miserable. Again. So she headed off
home on her own.

As she walked, a well-dressed man
came alongside.

'Good afternoon,' he said.

'Er, hi?' Esther said, speeding up a little.
She knew she shouldn't talk to strangers.

'Do you have somewhere important to be?' the man asked.

'Err, no.' Esther glanced back – her friends hadn't even noticed she had gone.

'It's just I saw you and thought, wow! Such natural beauty!'

'Me?'

'Humble too! Even better. How would you like to enter a competition, young lady? It doesn't cost anything, and the prize is to die for!'

'Sure,' Esther shrugged. 'What's the catch?'

'This is the catch!' snarled the man, grabbing her under one arm. He shoved a sack over her head, bundled her round the corner and dumped her into a cart filled with other scared young girls.

After a long, uncomfortable and frightening journey, Esther found herself in a camp in the middle of a thick, dark forest. The slippery man who had captured her was there too. She watched him eyeing all the other kidnapped girls huddled beside her. Then he rubbed his long, bony hands together and introduced himself as Haman, special advisor to the King. He was in charge of the competition: there would be months of treatments and tests leading to a grand beauty pageant, at which one of them would be crowned Queen of Iran!

Esther and the other girls shuddered at this terrible news. Three of them fainted onto the ground. One of them was sick in another girl's lap.

You see, the last Queen of Iran had mysteriously disappeared without a trace during a party. Some said the King was so angry with her for refusing to show off for his friends that he had fed her to his pet tigers. Others said that she was slowly rotting in a tiny cell deep below the palace. One report even claimed that the King had buried her alive under an old walnut tree in the courtyard. One thing was for sure: nobody wanted to be the next Queen of Iran.

Esther's days in the camp were long and hard.

6 a.m. Deep tissue pummel massage

7 a.m. History of Iran propaganda lecture

1 p.m. Ice bath endurance test

3 p.m. Silence for women workshop

5 p.m. 10-mile mud run

8 p.m. Exam: how to do what you are told and what to expect when you fail

If Esther ever forgot to turn up for a lesson, fell asleep during a treatment or flunked a test, she felt the full force of Haman's fury. He liked to shout at all the girls, telling them how useless they were before making them lick his boots clean.

On the last day, the King arrived. He checked each contestant like a farmer inspecting cows.

He pulled their teeth.

He sniffed their breath.

He stared at them,

and calculated how much value they would add to his kingdom.

At the end of the day, the King announced his champion.

'**Why me?**' Esther cried as she was carted off to the palace. '**It's not fair!**'

Many months later, Queen Esther was walking around the palace courtyard. She'd lost count of the number of times she had done it before. Life as a queen was dull and monotonous. She wasn't allowed to go anywhere or meet anyone. She hated it. How she wished she were back in her cold, dusty home with her uncle. She would never complain about him spoiling her fun again.

At that moment, just as Esther was walking past the old walnut tree, she heard a sound.

'**PSSST!**'

Queen Esther looked up from her daily trudge. It was just the security guard. Why would he be trying to get her attention?

'Oi! It's me!'

'Uncle?!' Esther said, her eyes lighting up. She skipped over to the gate. 'What are you doing here? If anyone sees you …? If anyone finds out you're my …! Oh, I'm so **happy** to see you again!'

After Esther had been kidnapped, her Uncle Mordecai had spent many months trying to track her down. When he had finally heard the news that she had been chosen to be the next Queen of Iran, he had cried for a week. Then, one morning, he wiped away his tears, put on his best suit, walked straight up to the palace and offered his services as a security guard – for free.

Esther smiled for the first time in a long time as she listened to his story. She still wished she could go back home, to the way things were, but having her uncle close by made her life slightly less unbearable.

It turned out that Mordecai was rather good at being a security guard. He kept a sharp eye on the King. He kept close watch on the Queen. Nobody broke in. Nothing got stolen.

Esther was learning how to survive as a queen too. She discovered that so long as she avoided the King, she could stay out of trouble. Weeks went by, and she began to hope that he had forgotten about her altogether.

Unfortunately, Haman was still very much on the scene. As special advisor to the King, he felt it was his job to keep the Queen in her place. Most days he made a point of visiting Esther with a bunch of insults or a sneery threat.

One morning, Haman marched into Esther's quarters in an even worse temper than usual.

'This is all your fault,' he said, shoving a newspaper in Esther's face.

On the front page was a huge picture of her Uncle Mordecai under the headline:

LUCKY ROYAL LOOKOUT UNCOVERS SECRET PLOT TO MURDER KING

Esther could feel the blood draining from her face. Had Haman found out that the hero of the hour was her uncle? Mordecai may have saved the King's life, but now Esther had a horrible feeling that her own life needed saving. She bit her lip and hid her fear behind her beautiful smile.

But the King's special advisor was angry for a different reason altogether.

'It's all your fault,' he said again. 'If you just got the King to notice you a bit more, then he might thank me for finding you. I am the real hero of the hour. I should be featured on the front page of the newspaper. Not stupid Mordecai. All he did was hear a little rumour.'

Esther froze. Maybe her secret was safe after all. But Mordecai wasn't.

'His luck has run out,' Haman continued, rolling a pair of Iranian dice around in the palm of his hand and then squeezing them hard in his fist. 'I will deal with him, and everyone close to him.'

Haman grabbed the paper and stomped out, muttering something about Iranians of Israeli origin. Esther was worried. She paced up and down her room, wishing once again that she was not the Queen of Iran.

Esther was still pacing up and down her room in the middle of the night when she heard a familiar noise.

'PSSST!'

'Uncle!' called Esther as she opened her little window and leaned out. 'Be quiet. You need to get out of here. Your life is in danger.'

Mordecai shrugged. 'ALL OUR LIVES ARE IN DANGER,' he shouted. 'Haman tricked the King into signing a royal decree: all Iranians of Israeli origin are to be slaughtered at the end of the month!'

Esther leaned against the wall. She knew that Haman would do something dastardly – but this was even more dastardly than she could possibly have imagined. There were thousands of people of Israeli origin living in Iran. It would be a bloodbath.

'Don't worry about me, Uncle,' Esther said at last. 'Nobody knows about my Israeli origins. Just look after yourself.' She

blew him a kiss and waited for him to blow one back before
disappearing.

But Mordecai was not going anywhere. Instead, he stood
there looking cross.

'Listen carefully, young lady,' he said, wagging his finger.
'This is not the time for looking after ourselves. This is the time
for looking after everyone else. Use your royal position for
something good: persuade the King to change the royal decree.'

Esther couldn't believe her ears. Nobody told the King what to do and got away with it. Especially queens. And definitely not queens of secret Israeli origin. Whatever had happened to her old Uncle Mordecai – her dreadfully, wonderfully overprotective Uncle Mordecai?

'Uncle, don't **you** care that the King might kill me on the spot for such a crime as this?'

'Oh Esther, don't **you** care that God might have put you in this very spot for **such a time as this?**'

Lying on her bed later that evening, wishing she were somewhere else, anywhere else, Esther decided to have a word with Mordecai's God.

Everything she'd ever wanted to say to him came flooding out: 'It's not fair that my parents died. It's not fair I was adopted. It's not fair that Haman kidnapped me. It's not fair that I am imprisoned in the palace. And it's not fair that my uncle wants me to risk my life to try to save your people. God, why have you allowed all these unfortunate things to happen to me?'

Esther didn't get a wink of sleep for three nights in a row. Each morning, the sun rose and she still felt in the dark. On the third morning she came to a conclusion: she had nothing left to lose.

As soon as she was dressed, Esther slipped past the guards, her heart racing. She could barely breathe as she edged her way to the door of the throne room. Her stomach churned as she stepped into the King's presence uninvited. She had broken three laws in three minutes. In another three minutes she could be dead.

The King looked shocked, then confused. Then, to her surprise, he beamed at her, beckoning her in with his royal sceptre.

'Queen Esther? This is a strange coincidence. I was just thinking about you. What do you wish for?'

Esther pinched herself, checked her head was still attached to her body and realised she hadn't even thought about what to do next.

'I wish to ask you … err … um … to dinner? Tonight? With Haman?'

That evening, Esther put on a sumptuous banquet and played the part of the perfect Iranian hostess beautifully. It went so well, she invited them back again the following evening.

If she played her cards right, Esther thought she might just get the chance to bring the dinner conversation round to the unpleasant subject of the slaughtering-of-people-like-her royal decree. She opened her window to see if she could spot Mordecai.

As luck would have it, just at that very moment Haman

and the King bumped into each other in the courtyard. Esther watched from behind her curtain, secretly listening in to their conversation.

'Your Majesty,' said Haman, bowing low. 'You don't mind if I hang someone today, do you? Just an annoying, worthless little security guard who nobody would miss. I've got some brand-new shiny gallows I want to test out.'

Esther clasped her hand over her mouth. Mordecai's life was in more danger than ever before. She would have to warn him just as soon as the coast was clear.

'Go ahead,' agreed the King, 'so long as your hanging doesn't interfere with my award ceremony this afternoon.'

'Award ceremony?' Haman's eyes lit up. 'Will my, err, I mean, this award ceremony include a parade? The royal robe? A crown? A procession of royal horses? Will there be crowds of people lining the streets, clapping and cheering me, err, I mean, cheering the lucky recipient of this award?'

'Great ideas, Haman!' said the King, patting Haman on the back. 'You are just the person ... to make all of those things happen – for this guy.'

The King pulled out an old newspaper and pointed. Esther nearly fell out of her window in surprise. On the front page was the huge picture of Mordecai!

'But … I thought …' stuttered Haman, scratching his head so hard Esther wondered if his brains would suddenly pop out. 'This guy? Really? Are you sure?'

The King scowled at Haman. 'Of course I'm sure, you imbecile. I'm the King. I'm always sure.'

Haman tried again: 'But … Your Majesty … This happened ages ago. Why award him now?'

'I don't know why I didn't see the newspaper at the time,' the King said. 'I just came across it last night when I couldn't sleep. It was buried under a pile of other paperwork. I don't know who put it there.'

'Err …' Haman said, before rushing off to organise the award ceremony.

As Esther got ready for the second dinner party with the King and Haman, she couldn't stop thinking about how Mordecai's life had been saved – literally under her nose.

'Well, it's not every day you find out your life has been saved,'
the King said later as he laid back on Queen Esther's rugs and
tucked into his starters.

Haman slurped his soup. He looked as sick as an Iranian parrot who'd eaten too many fig rolls.

'It was a wonderful award ceremony,' the King said, eyeing up the mouth-watering main courses all laid out on gold plates. 'Mordecai couldn't have been more surprised.'

Haman nearly choked on a pickled olive. He still couldn't believe he had spent the day parading Mordecai around town like a hero instead of executing him on his new gallows.

'This country needs more Mordecais,' said the King, smothering his sweetmeats with extra cream. 'We can't have people plotting to murder us now, can we?'

Haman's face was now so red he looked like he was about to explode.

The King didn't notice. He only had eyes for his puddings. After his seventh helping he smacked his lips and patted his stomach.

'Let me grant you a wish, Queen Esther,' he said, 'as a thank you for such a wonderful evening. What would you like? A ring? An extra room in the palace? Half the kingdom?'

This was Esther's moment. A now-or-never, life-or-death, do-or-die moment. She took a deep breath.

'Your Majesty, I wish to ask you to help people like me … to not get murdered.'

'**What?**' asked the King.

'I mean …' Esther couldn't turn back now. 'Mordecai, the man you honoured today, happens to be of Israeli origin. As do I. There are many people like us in your kingdom. We are all to be slaughtered because of your royal decree.'

'Why would I sign such an evil decree?' The King picked up his royal goblet.

Esther wondered if he were about to throw it at her.

'Because, Your Majesty, you were tricked into it – by …'

'By whom?'

Esther sat up and pointed at the other dinner guest in the room.

'**Haman?**' The King spat out his wine. '**Is this true?**'

'Me? I had no idea the Queen was …'

Esther felt Haman's eyes glaring at her. Then suddenly he lunged at her. She had a sudden flashback to when she was a young girl. When someone had grabbed her, pulled a sack over her head and changed her world.

'I should have killed you when I had the chance,' Haman whispered in Esther's ear.

'Security!' called the King. 'The Queen is being attacked!'

It was actually Haman, not
Mordecai, who ended the day
hanging on those shiny
brand-new gallows. And it was
Mordecai, not Haman, who got
his picture in the newspaper the next day.

LUCKY ROYAL
LOOKOUT
BECOMES KING'S
NEW SPECIAL
ADVISOR!

That week, there were a lot of celebrations. All around the country, families and friends of those of Israeli origin put on big parties where they told each other the story of how Esther – against all the odds – had persuaded the King to do what kings never do – and change a royal decree.

After that, life for Esther continued much as before. Each day she trudged around the palace courtyard and hoped that the King wouldn't bother her. But now at least she had something to look forward to. Every day, her uncle would pop by her quarters on his way home from work and tell her all the news. Esther could always hear him coming as he sang a little song to himself.

I imagine it went something like this:

Hallelujah! Iranian men
And women of Israeli origin.
Your God made Esther your Queen
For such a time as this. Amen.

The incredible rescue is still celebrated today in a global annual Jewish festival called Purim, after Haman's Iranian dice. No matter how unfair or unfortunate life seems to be, God is always in control. Read the story for yourself in the book of Esther.

THE CENTURION

THE TALE OF THE ITALIAN INVADER WHO FOUGHT AN UNEXPECTED BATTLE

WELCOME TO ITALY

Italy has been home to plenty of geniuses over the centuries. There was Leonardo da Vinci who invented the first concept flying machine as well as painting the world's favourite portrait. There was Galileo, a scientist who mastered the telescope and discovered that the planets revolve around the sun. Perhaps you have heard of Antonio Vivaldi the brilliant composer, Marco Polo, the great explorer, or Giorgio Armani, the well-known fashion creator.

Italian geniuses over the centuries have invented roads,

designed toilet systems, painted elaborate church ceilings, engineered supercars, built a tower that leaned, and brought the world pizza and pasta.

Italians used to be brilliant at invading too. They conquered countries from Britain in the North to Africa in the South, from Spain in the East to Turkey in the West. They stationed troops throughout their empire to impose laws, collect taxes and execute rebels. It is fair to say that these Italian geniuses were not very popular, as you will see in this tale.

The centurion was staring at his reflection in the mirror as he was getting dressed.

'I want a war!' he shouted as he buckled his regulation army belt tightly around his waist. 'Or at least a battle or two.'

He grabbed his breastplate and strapped it on.

'If I don't get out of this sleepy lakeside town, I'll die of boredom,' he sighed, and pulled on his shoes.

Finally, he dropped his helmet onto his head and gave his sword a nice, big swing.

'What a waste of my military training!' he grumbled.

With all his uniform on, the centurion looked extremely fierce and frightening. He could **skewer** you with that sharp sword and **toast** you over a fire like a marshmallow. He could **headbutt** you like a football halfway across town with that helmet and you wouldn't remember a thing. Those shoes would **crush** all the bones in your poor foot even if he accidentally stamped on it. Although he probably would do it quite on purpose and without an apology. His breastplate protected his heart of steel. He didn't care about anyone.

The centurion lived for two things. The first thing he lived for was to **follow** orders.

He only got washed and dressed in the morning because Caesar ordered it.

He only ate three meals a day because Caesar ordered it.

He only stayed in Capernaum far away from his Italian home because Caesar ordered it.

If Caesar had ordered him to jump off a cliff, stab his own eye or cross the road without looking he would have done it. An order was an order.

The other thing he lived for was to **give** orders.

Every day he ordered his many servants to do this, do that and do the other.

Every day he commanded his 100 soldiers to march here and march there and march here and there again.

If he had ordered them to juggle with beehives, stick sticks in their ears or dangle upside down off a tall tree they would have done it. The centurion made sure they all knew that an order was an order was an order.

The centurion had been waiting for a new order from Caesar for days. For weeks. For months. If he were Caesar he would sit in his Italian villa and issue orders left, right and centre. Wage a war here. Bring on a battle there. Campaigns. Crusades. Conflicts. Skirmishes. Squabbles. Scuffles. Just one word of one of these just once and the centurion would leap into action and put Capernaum on the map.

But there was no word. The last thing the centurion had heard from Caesar was ages ago: 'Stay where you are. I'll keep you posted'. It was so infuriating.

Centurions with orders are pretty dangerous. So are centurions with no orders, as the people of Capernaum were about to discover. The war-starved centurion decided to go pick some fights of his own, starting with a bunch of fishermen mending their nets after a long night on the lake.

'Oi! You! Stinky pile of festering fish guts! Caught anything recently? A **cold?** A **terrible disease?'**

The fishermen friends bit their lips. They had not caught enough fish to pay the taxes they owed the centurion, let alone feed their families.

'Don't look so drippy! There'll be no sitting around knitting while I'm in charge. Go and catch more fish – so you can pay me more taxes. You've been warned.'

The poor tired fishermen waited until the centurion had marched round the corner before slinking back into their boats. If only someone would save them from these greedy Italian invaders.

The rampaging centurion burst into the local synagogue where the religious leaders were holding an emergency meeting.

'Oi! You! Ugly bunch of **boneless bumblers!**'

The rabbis paused their discussion on how to fund the urgent repair work needed. They didn't have any solutions.

'I see your holy building is very holey. I wouldn't bother fixing it if I were you. One word from Caesar and it'll be a pile of rubble along with your jobs before you can say "Ecclesiastes".'

The next target for the centurion was in the marketplace. As he paraded through, the noisy town square fell silent. Nobody liked him and nobody trusted him. He helped himself to a bunch of grapes and opened his huge mouth to deliver some more tasty insults.

'Oi! You! Pathetic pack of **pitiful peasants.**'

Nobody dared say a word.

'Don't look at me like that. I'm here to fight poverty for you. Just pick me out a poor person and I'll beat him up.'

The townsfolk didn't see the funny side.

'Oh, cheer up – money can't buy happiness. The best things

in life are free. Like these grapes – mmm!
Oh, and him!'

The centurion walked
over to a boy cowering
behind his family fish stall.

'Oi! You!
Miserable morsel
of a boy! Come
with me.'

The centurion
grabbed the lad by the
ear and dragged him

away. 'Your family is just being selfish getting you to sell fish for
them. You're going to work for me now. It's an offer you can't
refuse.'

The poor boy's parents fell to their knees and begged the
centurion to reconsider. This was their one and only son who
they loved. He wasn't old enough to leave home yet. Their
business would go under without him. But it was too late. The
centurion dragged the boy all the way back to his barracks and
ordered the gardener to set him to work.

The barracks were quieter than usual. The centurion was puzzled. He didn't remember giving his men a day off. This wasn't the Italian Riviera where they could just swan around like tourists. They were supposed to be polishing their armour and practising their drill. But the only person to be seen was the gardener.

'Oi! You! **Weedy old prune-faced dirtball!** Where have all my soldiers gone?'

The gardener pointed one of his green fingers to the mountain on the edge of town.

When the centurion looked up, he saw what seemed to be a huge crowd of people gathered on the hillside. He stomped off to shout at them and enforce a new rule he'd just made up: **No Picnics.**

The crowd was further up the
hill than they appeared from the
bottom, and the centurion was
slowed down by his heavy armour.
When he finally reached the top of
the hill, he had to sit down to catch
his breath. He almost wished he'd brought a picnic.

The centurion could hear a man teaching at the opposite
side of the slope. Everyone was listening intently to him as he
described a kingdom that sounded nothing like Caesar's.

This new kingdom was topsy-turvy – the least important
people got the best VIP treatment. The centurion did not like
the sound of that at all.

But it was about to get a whole lot worse.

The centurion watched as the poor fishermen he had
picked a fight with earlier got a special mention by the teacher,
along with the promise that they would be first to see the new
kingdom. Then the rabbis he'd insulted were promised a special
place in the new kingdom too. Even the crying parents of the
boy the centurion had stolen from the market got a promise of
comfort.

The centurion was furious. This teacher was deliberately undoing all his menacing. The people of Capernaum didn't need encouraging, comforting and inspiring. They needed to know their place. Who did this teacher think he was?

The centurion tried launching some insults at him, but the light breeze and strange acoustics of the valley carried them away in the opposite direction. Nobody even turned round.

But the teacher still hadn't finished. The next people to get a shout-out were the soldiers. The centurion's own missing soldiers! They were being blessed by the teacher for being peacemakers for God's new kingdom! This was beyond belief!

The centurion felt a wave of panic. Something was terribly wrong here. His men were supposed to be warriors loyal to him. Not peacemakers loyal to God. If Caesar found out …

The centurion suddenly found himself feeling as worried as all the people he had menaced that day. He could lose his income, like the fishermen he had overtaxed. He could lose his job, like the rabbis he had insulted. He could lose his home, like the boy he had stolen from the market. His life would be over.

Finally, the centurion had himself a battle. It wasn't the battle he had expected or asked for that morning. It was an invisible war raging on the wrong side of his armour.

Beneath his helmet, his head spun with thoughts about what was right and what was wrong.

Beneath his belt his stomach knotted up. The thought of Caesar, who he had once worshipped, now made him feel sick.

Behind his shield, his steel heart softened. Now he knew how those people he had bullied had felt.

He looked at his boots. Perhaps his life needed a new direction after all.

As the centurion headed back down the hill, he passed a small pool. Looking at his reflection in the water, he threw the last insults of his life.

'Oi! You! Sorry Excuse For A Centurion. Or should I call you a **Sin-turion?** You thought your jokes were funny? Well, those punchlines have now punched you right back where it hurts. The new you has given the old you its marching orders.'

Then the centurion made a list of all the new orders he intended to make as soon as he got home.

1. Lower the taxes. Apologise to the fishermen.
2. Give a large donation to the synagogue. Apologise to the rabbis.
3. Return the boy. Apologise to the parents.

'Signore!' The centurion looked up to see his gardener running towards him. He looked worried.

'Something terrible has happened. The servant boy you stole, I mean, borrowed, is dying. The doctors can't save him, and his parents are nowhere to be found!'

The centurion found himself feeling something he had never ever felt before. He used to get a kick out of watching people die slow, painful deaths. Suddenly he wanted more than anything for this boy to live. But he was powerless. Even if the whole of the Roman army turned up with Caesar in person it would be no good. The boy needed a miracle. If only he knew of someone who could help him get a message to God …

The centurion turned around again and headed back up the hill. It wasn't long before he came face to face with the man he wanted to see – the teacher, who was leading the crowd back into town.

'Well, catch a load of that!' said the fishermen, as they watched the centurion fall to his knees in respect.

'We don't believe it!' said the rabbis, as the centurion begged the teacher to help the dying boy.

'OUR BOY IS DYING!' cried the parents of the boy from the market.

The centurion explained to the teacher everything that had happened that day.

'Please just give the order,' the centurion sighed. 'I don't deserve you to come to my house, but my servant has done nothing wrong. One word from you and I know God will heal him.'

The centurion waited. He saw the boy's parents, the fisherman and the rabbis all staring at him in disgust. They were probably hoping the teacher would ban him from his new kingdom, or push him down the hill, or make him vanish back to Italy. But the teacher did none of those things. He looked in amazement at the centurion.

'Oi! you! Shining example of a faith-warrior! Incredible role model of the people! Courageous champion of the world! One day you will be welcomed to a celebration banquet in my new kingdom. A great battle has been fought here today and victory has been won because you believed!'

'Did you hear what the teacher just said?' the surprised rabbis asked the centurion. 'He basically said you had more faith than us – and we thought we had plenty of faith!'

'And he said that you had more guts than us,' added the fishermen, nodding their heads in respect. 'And we definitely have guts.'

The boys' parents ran over.

'Does this mean that our son might be OK after all?'

The centurion watched the crowd disappear down the road towards his house and sat down on a small clump of grass. He would follow later. Now that he had done what he could for the boy, he felt, for the first time in his life, like he wanted to enjoy the peace.

'Oi! You!'

It was a week later and the centurion was in the marketplace again. He paid for his bunch of grapes and walked over to the fish stall. The boy grinned from ear to ear when he saw him.

'Don't worry,' he said. 'I'm still alive!'

The centurion had been checking on him every day –
sometimes twice.

'Any orders from Caesar today?' the boy teased.

'Who cares?' laughed the centurion. 'Maybe he pasta way!
Passed away? I'm dead funny!'

'Oh, I've got one!' the boy said. 'Do you know what I saw at
the end of your army the other day? Your handy!'

The centurion laughed and slapped the boy on the back.
Very gently. 'I heard there is going to be another talk on the
mountain in a bit. Grab a sardine sandwich and we can go hear
the teacher together!'

'Do I finally get to meet the miracle man who healed me?'
the boy asked. 'You have to tell me more about him.'

'Well,' said the centurion, 'my men tell me he is from
Nazareth originally, but I think there's more to it. He speaks
about God like he actually knows him. He sees what's really
inside people, not just what's on the outside. And he's given me
a hope for a future that's really worth fighting for. I'd love to
introduce him to you. **His name is Jesus.'**

This story can be read in Matthew 5 and 8. You can find out more about Jesus in the other books of the Bible, but especially Matthew, Mark, Luke and John. You can even meet him yourself. Ask someone who knows him to introduce you to him.

THE SENATOR

THE TALE OF THE SUDANESE SENATOR
WHO MADE A SPLASH

WELCOME TO SUDAN

MUSEUM ARCHAEOLOGY

When Jesus was alive, Sudan, along with much of central Africa was known as the rich and powerful empire of Ethiopia and it stretched so far that many considered it to be the end of the world.

Today, we are still making archaeological discoveries that tell us more about this powerful and lavish empire. The massive Ethiopian Empire is no more, and today Sudan is the third largest country in Africa and currently one of the poorest in the world. It is also one of the hottest and driest countries, with half of it classed as desert.

Although some parts of Sudan have good access to water, much of the country suffers from water shortages. Sometimes the only sources of water for miles around are dirty ponds and ditches. Children who have to spend time collecting water often end up missing school. Sometimes the water makes them really sick.

Despite life being so difficult in Sudan, the churches are growing, and many people are becoming Christians. This is the exciting story of the first African to become a follower of Jesus.

Have you ever been to a theme park and queued up for a ride only to find out that you are not quite tall enough to be allowed on?

Have you ever wanted to watch a movie or play a video game and been told that you aren't old enough?

Perhaps you've sat on the subs bench for a whole match and never made it onto the pitch.

If anyone has ever told you that you are **too short,** or **too young,** or **too slow,** or just not **good enough**, then you probably know exactly how one visitor felt many years ago in Jerusalem when he wanted to visit the temple but was told 'NO ENTRY'.

'Why? Do you think I'm not rich enough?' the visitor asked the officer blocking the doorway. The visitor

was a tall, slim man, dressed in
a flamboyant tunic and grand,
designer headwrap, which made
him appear even taller. But the
most striking thing about him
was his gold rings. Not only
were they on his fingers, but on
his clothes as well. He looked
like a walking jewellery store.

The sour-faced officer tapped the entry requirements notice
on the door, before folding his arms across his broad chest.

'No entry! Rules are rules!'

'Perhaps you think I'm not important enough?'
the rich man said, casually waving at his driver standing by the
most expensive chariot the city had ever seen.

The officer shook his head.

'Perhaps you think I'm not smart enough?'

The other visitors in the queue raised their eyebrows. They
had already heard him around the town speaking and reading
several languages fluently. He was clearly better educated than
the rest of them put together.

There was only one thing left. He took a deep breath.

'Perhaps you think I'm not man enough?'

The officer gave the slightest of nods and a hint of a smirk. 'Rules are rules!' he repeated.

The tall, important, rich, smart, but unwelcome visitor raised his voice. He wanted everyone to hear just how upset and offended he was.

'I may have no beard. I may have a high-pitched voice. I may not be married or have children. But no man is more dedicated to queen and country than me. I, Senator of Sudan, Treasurer of the Queen of Candace, Member of the Sudanese Royal Court, Assigned Eunuch, guest of your government, have just been at the palace negotiating the transnational trade deal of the century. Are you man enough to do that?! WELL, ARE YOU?!'

The bustling temple plaza fell silent. Everyone was watching. The officer twitched as the senator addressed the frozen crowds of Jerusalem.

'In all my days of travelling I have never been refused entry anywhere. This, Jerusalem, is an outrage.

Beware the wrath of Sudan.'

With that, the snubbed senator swept down the steps and straight into his waiting chariot. Maybe he would tear up that trade deal. Perhaps he would send some Sudanese soldiers to terrorise the town. He could even wage full-out war!

Now, it was usual for a sudden surge of street vendors to descend on any visitors seen leaving the temple. They knew all the tricks in the book to make money out of tourists, especially rich, important ones. But seeing how angry the senator was, nobody dared go anywhere near him.

Except for one brave, young girl. As Jerusalem watched in surprise, she walked straight up to the chariot, curtseyed politely and placed a huge, ornate souvenir in the senator's lap.

'Good afternoon, sir,' the girl said. 'You are holding in your hands the longest and most wonderful scroll we have. Originally written by Isaiah the prophet, the words are over seven hundred years old and are the founding principles for the temple. My father spent a whole year copying it by hand with nothing but the finest inks from around the world.'

'Are you crazy, girl?' The senator picked up the souvenir and held it out to her. 'Didn't you just see the way I was treated? You can take your scroll and your temple and your rules and …'

'The rules are wrong!' the scroll-seller interrupted in a quiet voice.

'What did you say?'

'The rules are wrong! I've tried telling the temple leaders, but they shoo me away because I am a girl. It's right here in this scroll.'

She pushed it back into his lap.

'You should read it, sir. It will change your life.'

The senator looked the girl up and down. She seemed too young and too poor to have been educated. 'Do you really expect me to believe **you** have read this enormous scroll?'

'I've read all the scrolls!' the girl said proudly. 'I read the texts aloud to my father as he writes. If we get one letter wrong, the whole scroll gets destroyed. We're very precise. Read chapter 56 for yourself. You'll see I'm right. They should have let you into the temple.'

The senator smiled as he imagined the temple leaders with their long beards and their fixed rules being outsmarted by this girl.

He pulled out of his tunic the bag of gold he had been planning on generously donating to the temple and handed the whole lot to the scroll-seller. It was more than she would have expected to earn in a lifetime.

As the elephants led the chariot away, he glanced back to see the surprised look on everyone's faces. Sure enough, it had got everyone talking.

The senator smiled smugly to himself, made himself comfortable for the long, boring journey back to Sudan and opened the scroll at chapter 1.

Many, many hours and 51 chapters later his head ached. He'd come across: gobbling graves, fiery angels, wars and battles, soaring eagles, serpents and sea monsters, smoking cities, flattened mountains, even dead people coming back to life.

It was the weirdest thing he had ever read. What did it all mean?

The scroll-seller girl would know, he was sure of it. But going back to Jerusalem now would mean travelling in the dark. Travelling in the dark was dangerous. There might be bandits. He would stay in Gaza tonight, then tomorrow he would go straight back to Jerusalem for the answers to all his questions.

The senator carried on reading his strange scroll. He hadn't got any further than chapter 53 when he heard a noise behind him. Someone was shouting. Someone was running towards him. Someone was after him.

'Faster! Faster!' the senator shouted to the driver.

'Bandit alert!'

If you ever plan on being chased by a bandit on the road from Jerusalem to Gaza, think very carefully about what sort of chariot you might need. Horses are good. Camels are surprisingly fast. Elephants are not such a good idea.

Elephants have two gears. Slow. And slightly less slow. That's why, despite going as fast as they could, the bandit was gaining on them.

The bandit looked rough. His clothes were covered in dust. He looked like he'd never had a bath in his life. He looked like the sort of person who survived by the skin of his rotten teeth by robbing rich senators and leaving them for dead by the side of the road. And this bandit looked like he didn't even care about doing it in broad daylight.

Soon he was so close that the senator could see the man's hair sticking out at all angles. He could hear him muttering under his breath. He could even smell the sweat that was pouring off him.

The senator shoved the scroll up his tunic just as the bandit jumped on board.

'No entry!' the senator cried out quickly. 'Rules are rules! By authority of the Queen of Sudan. Get out of here!'

To his great surprise, the bandit began **laughing**.

'Is that the way you treat all your guests? Am I not good enough for you?'

'Perhaps you think I am too dirty?' The bandit blew some dust off his tunic.

'Perhaps you think I am too sweaty?' He wiped

his head with his sleeve and blew his nose on it.

'Or perhaps I am too late? Have you finished the scroll already?'

'Scroll? What scroll? I haven't got any scroll!' lied the even-more-surprised senator, clutching his precious bundle tightly behind his crossed arms.

'Very funny! The scroll of Isaiah can be so tricky to understand. My name is Philip, and I am a teacher. I am an expert in history, prophecy and theology. Ask me anything!'

The senator scratched his head. He'd never heard of a bandit who introduced himself by name and specialist subject.

The possibility occurred to the senator that he may have badly misjudged this bandit. Experts in the scrolls seemed to be coming his way in very strange shapes and sizes. First one that was a street-trader girl. Then one that looked like a bandit! He slowly pulled the scroll out from under his tunic and opened it on chapter 53.

'I was up to here. The bit about a man who was rather misunderstood. What do you make of that?'

'Oh, I know him! That's Jesus.'

'Jesus! Who's Jesus?'

For the next hour, Philip told the senator all about Jesus: his life, his teaching, his miracles. He explained how Jesus went to Jerusalem where the temple officers not only shunned him but tortured him and killed him too. Then he showed the senator where the prophet predicted that Jesus would save the world and that God would raise him from the dead.

'All this came true? In my lifetime?'

This Isaiah lesson was blowing the senator's mind.

'Boy, those temple officers are stupid. They murdered the very person their own scrolls predicted would come and save them. Who would be so dumb as to think that the very one sent to help was a common criminal to be afraid of?'

'Remind you of anyone?' Philip laughed.

The senator's face reddened. 'I'm sorry I thought you were

a bandit. You're right. I'm no better than those temple officers. Maybe I didn't deserve to be let into the temple after all. That reminds me! The scroll-seller told me to read chapter 56 – what does that bit say?'

Philip showed the senator that it was all about eunuchs and visitors from other countries, and how one day they wouldn't be locked out of the temple any more. He explained that God never judges people based on how rich, or important, or smart, or man enough they are. Because of Jesus, God himself had torn down the entry requirements and put up a big 'ALL WELCOME' sign.

The senator was thrilled! The scroll-seller was right – this was life-changing!

The senator suddenly remembered a day as a boy, when his

parents had put a little 'ALL WELCOME' sign outside their house. There had been a big party, and a ceremony where he had promised a lifetime of loyalty to the Queen of Sudan. The senator winced as he thought about it and wondered if there were a ceremony for people who chose to dedicate their life to be loyal to God.

'Jesus taught the ceremony of baptism,' Philip replied.

'What's that?'

'You go underwater – just for a moment – to recognise that we can never measure up to the rules. And then you get pulled up again – to symbolise being welcomed into God's family.'

The senator jumped up and hugged the bandit-teacher who had brought him such good news. 'Stop the chariot!'

Somehow, in the middle of this desert road, the chariot

came to a stop right next to a waterhole! Both the senator and Philip gasped in surprise. The elephants could hardly believe it either. They waded in for a shower as the senator removed his jewellery and headdress.

Only a few weeks earlier the senator had imagined his first prayer to God would be in the temple on a tourist trip. But it ended up being by the side of a road in a muddy pool.

'Why did you just take a bath in a ditch?' the driver asked the senator as he wrung dirty water out of his tunic. 'Now you look as rough as that bandit. You can't go back to Jerusalem looking like that!'

'We don't need Jerusalem any more,' the senator said. 'We are going straight to Sudan. We've got to tell the other eunuchs this good news. And the Queen. And the royal court. And everyone else in the whole of Africa. Right, Philip?'

The driver and the senator looked everywhere but it seemed Philip had disappeared as strangely as he had arrived.

'That's a shame,' the senator said to the driver as he climbed back into the chariot. 'I wanted to know more about the Holy Spirit. I wonder if he is mentioned at all in the rest of the scroll?'

By the time the senator arrived in Gaza, he had read the whole scroll. There was a lot he still didn't understand but one thing was sure, it wasn't going to end up in the Queen's Museum of Foreign Artefacts next to all the other souvenirs he had brought back from his travels. He was going to take care of this himself and would not rest until everyone had heard its good news.

You can read this story of the first African convert to Christianity in Acts 8. Read Acts for yourself to discover where Philip disappeared to, and how the Holy Spirit can help you tell the world about the good news of God's welcome.

BARNABAS

THE TALE OF THE CYPRIOT SLEUTH
WHO UNLOCKED A MYSTERY

WELCOME TO CYPRUS

Cyprus is a beautiful Mediterranean island. You could say it is an island of two halves. On the one hand there are ancient archaeological sites, and on the other it is also full of brand-new luxury resorts. Half of the landscape is craggy mountains to be climbed; the other half is sandy beaches to relax on. Eucalyptus trees reach up to the sky while sea turtles dive down under the blue water. Designer

boutiques can be found next door to traditional market stalls. In some places the sea has carved gorges, while in others it has created lagoons. Half the country speaks Turkish, the other half speak Greek.

God likes to bring very different people together. In this story the kind and clever man from Cyprus is about to meet someone very different and very dangerous. If his deductions are correct.

B arnabas' house was the strangest house on Butcher Street. For a start, the front door was always unlocked – even in the middle of the night. If a key had ever existed, it had long since disappeared into the mysterious place where unused keys end up. There was also an enormous sign hanging on the wall which, once upon a time, had said 'DO NOT DISTURB'. The 'NOT' was not there any more. It had been firmly scratched out. That was why there was always a queue of people waiting outside.

Everyone knew that if you lived in Jerusalem just under two thousand years ago and you had a problem, or a mystery that needed solving, Barnabas of Butcher Street was just the person for the job.

If you had an argument with your brother – then your parents sent you to Barnabas to get to the bottom of things. If your lunch money

had been stolen – Barnabas
would discover who was
responsible. If you couldn't do
your homework – Barnabas
could always deduce the
answers. If your pet tortoise
wouldn't come out of his
shell – Barnabas knew how to

persuade him. If it was going to rain on your birthday party –
Barnabas could bring the sunshine instead. (Well, OK, maybe
not the last two – but you get the picture.)

Barnabas didn't mind what you had or hadn't done. He
didn't mind what had or hadn't been done to you. He welcomed
everyone. His motto was: **'Any Time. Any Crime.'**

He had helped to solve the case of the missing magician. He
had cracked the case of the corrupt courtiers. And he had been
there at the big reveal of the mysterious Jerusalem jailbreak.

Barnabas never charged even a penny for his services. But if
you ended up spending any time with him, you would quickly
discover that what he liked most was the opportunity to bore
you senseless with the wonders of his birthplace.

Then you would have to listen to him describe each of the 20 rare species of orchids to be found in Cyprus, or some of the 371 types of bird native to the island, or the unique features of the mouflon sheep, or the various routes up Mount Olympus.

After that, he would tell you about the whitewashed houses nestled in green hills, the sun-kissed beaches that merged into blue oceans, and how the friendly villagers connected along dusty footpaths, swapping pots of olive oil or gossip.

Barnabas could talk about the beauties of Cyprus until the cows came home, or perhaps until the mouflon sheep came home.

One morning, Barnabas was sitting in his armchair, surrounded by books and papers, dreaming of Cyprus and waiting for his next visitor when John-Mark ran in.

John-Mark was his trouble-prone nephew. He used to visit his uncle for help so often, Barnabas joked that he might as well move into Butcher Street with him. So he did. Anyone else would have thrown him straight out again, but Barnabas wasn't anyone else.

'Uncle, you're not going to believe this,' John-Mark said, rushing over to the window.

'There's ... nobody ... outside!'

A puzzled look crossed Barnabas' face. He looked out of his window and, sure enough, Butcher Street, usually bustling with people and problems galore, was ominously deserted.

'Mrs Hebron! Come quick!' Barnabas called, sitting down again.

Mrs Hebron was the housekeeper – a short lady with a short temper to match. Barnabas didn't need a housekeeper, but nobody else would hire her. He always found a couple of things for her  to do each day to keep her feeling useful.

'There you are, Mrs Hebron. Do you know why nobody is waiting to see me today?'

'Oh, haven't you heard?' the housekeeper said, rolling her eyes. 'You were probably too busy dreaming about Cyprus with its stupid beaches, stupid palm trees and stupid sunsets. Some of us live in the real world, you know.'

'Thank you for that helpful reminder, Mrs Hebron, but what exactly haven't I heard?'

'The rumour. Everyone's talking about it. They say Saul is on his way to Butcher Street – to butcher us.'

'Saul!' gasped John-Mark. 'Saul the Serial Killer? Saul the Slaughterer? SAUL AS IN IT'S "SAUL" OVER FOR US?'

'See what you've done there, Barnabas,' the housekeeper added. 'We're all going to die and it's all your fault! You and your front door that doesn't lock.' Mrs Hebron and her bad temper disappeared outside, slamming the unlockable door behind them.

Barnabas picked up the newspaper while John-Mark hopped from one foot to another. He looked even more terrified than usual.

'Uncle, this is terrible! Saul must have found out about our secret church meetings. We need to get out of here! Why are you just sitting there reading the paper like nothing is wrong?'

Barnabas looked up. 'Mark my words, John-Mark. This may not be as bad as it sounds. In fact, this might even be good news. Please fetch Judas.'

'FIRST SAUL! NOW JUDAS!? ARE YOU PLANNING ON INVITING KING HEROD FOR LUNCH NEXT?' John-Mark screamed.

He grabbed Barnabas' cloak and pulled a face at the thought of all the local baddies descending on Butcher Street. 'Why not have Pontius Pilate over for tea too? We could betray ourselves, cart ourselves off to prison, organise our own trial, find each other guilty and arrange our own execution!'

'Calm down, John-Mark!'

'So you don't want me to fetch Judas the Betrayer?'

'I want you to fetch **Judas the Damascan**

– from Straight Street Church in Syria.' Barnabas tapped a

Judas

newspaper on his pile. 'There's an international medical convention in town. If I'm right, you'll find him staying in the hotel right around the corner.'

Ten minutes later, Barnabas and Judas the Damascan were sitting in Butcher Street laughing together over old memories,

while John-Mark hid under the travelling cloak looking terrified.

'Barnabas – I remember your first ever case!' Judas said.

'Ah – the Case of The Missing Body in the Garden.'

'I tell everyone I meet that story. Dead body. Sealed tight in a stone tomb. Guarded by the best Roman soldiers in town. And yet it vanishes. Leaving the grave clothes folded tidily. That mystery had everyone baffled for days.'

'To be fair,' Barnabas admitted, 'I was baffled too until witnesses came forward. And, of course, the whole thing was staring us in the face.' He picked up a book from his coffee table and held it up. 'There was only one possible logical explanation.'

'He rose from the dead!' the two men announced together chuckling.

'If it weren't for Jesus rising from the dead we would never have met,' Judas said.

'If it weren't for Jesus we wouldn't be in this mess,' John-Mark interrupted from under the cloak. 'And how can you two laugh at a time like this?'

'That reminds me, Judas,' Barnabas said, giving his nephew an encouraging nod. 'I wanted to ask you some questions. First of all: did a stranger knock on your door in Damascus three years ago – on the night of 13 August – and ask for help?'

'Barnabas, you clever old soul. How did you know?' Judas leaned forward in the chair to admire his friend.

'Yes, Uncle! How did you know?'

'Elementary, my dear fellows.' Barnabas flicked through a pile of newspapers until he found the one he was looking for. 'Here it is – 13 August.'

Barnabas blew the dust off the paper and pointed to the picture on the front page. Saul was sitting on a horse and looking fierce, with the headline,

Judas gulped as he remembered that day. 'We thought we were goners. Best-case scenario, we'd have been left in jail to rot. But we knew he'd probably have stoned us to death on the spot.'

'Yet you're still alive,' Barnabas mused. 'And no more mention of Saul in the daily news. The killer seemed to have disappeared and the papers conveniently forgot about him.'

'I wish I could conveniently forget him,' grumbled John-Mark to himself.

'I deduce that he must have had some sort of personal crisis,' Barnabas announced. 'One the local authorities were embarrassed to admit. One the church had to keep quiet about. That leads me to my second question: when Saul arrived at your door – was he disabled in some way?'

Judas grinned. His old friend's deductions were spot on again. He explained to Barnabas that when he opened the door and saw Saul, he grabbed a large pot to smash down on his head. He wasn't going to let that villain arrest his wife and children.

'But I couldn't do it Barnabas,' Judas admitted. 'He was blind!'

'I knew it!' Barnabas laughed, slamming his hands down on the table. 'God made sure he went to your house first. Nobody else in the whole of Damascus would have even noticed, let alone cared.'

'I wouldn't have cared,' John-Mark piped up. 'Eyes or no eyes, I'd have finished him off.'

'So, what did you do next?' Barnabas asked.

'I invited him in. Offered him dinner! Made up the spare room. My family thought I'd gone mad! He had to keep explaining to us how Jesus himself had appeared to him in a bright light and how he had seen the error of his ways.'

'Seen the error of his ways – with no eyes?' John-Mark was still sceptical.

Barnabas had one last question. 'Where did he go after you helped him escape?'

'You helped him escape?!' John-Mark shook his head. He would have done things very differently.

'Of course! The authorities wanted him dead as soon as he started telling people that he had met Jesus.'

'So, let me guess,' Barnabas said. 'You hid him in a basket and lowered him by rope down the outside wall in the middle of the night?'

'Exactly! It was the only way. I hope you don't mind that I gave him your address. Nobody else would have believed his story. But I don't understand why he never made it.'

Judas went back to his medical convention, puzzling it over. Meanwhile, Barnabas took John-Mark to visit Peter, their church leader.

Mrs Hebron promptly locked herself in the bathroom for the rest of the day.

Peter's house was full of very scared people. Everyone was talking at once, comparing notes on who had seen Saul lurking around Butcher Street. There seemed to be some disagreement over his disguises, but they were all convinced that if the killer really was looking for Barnabas, they were most certainly next on his hit list.

Barnabas coughed and waited for the hubbub to die down, before addressing the crowd. 'I need you all to know that, no matter what Saul has done, I will welcome him in. Remember my motto: *"Any time. Any crime."* '

Shockwaves rippled around the room. They were used to Barnabas' unlocked door but this was ridiculous! Everyone started talking and waving their arms around again. Barnabas was an idiot. Saul hated the church with a vengeance. He would arrest them all immediately. He would watch them die slowly with a smug smile on his face.

Suddenly there was a **loud KNOCK.** Everyone JUMPED.

Then everyone **tried** to hide.

Then everyone **realised** they couldn't hide.

Then everyone **moaned** about there being nowhere to hide.

'Stop!' Barnabas shouted. 'Remember. If Jesus can forgive those who tried to murder him, then we must do the same.'

Barnabas unbolted the door and opened it wide.

There stood Saul.

'You should have seen their faces!' John-Mark told Mrs Hebron later that evening, back in Butcher Street.

Mrs Hebron said nothing. She was too busy keeping an eye on Saul.

'It took ages for Barnabas and Saul to convince everyone he just wanted to be welcomed into church as a believer.'

'What I still don't understand,' Judas said to Saul, tucking

into his supper, 'is why you ended up at Peter's house after I gave you this address.'

Saul looked embarrassed. 'I was just too scared to knock. I thought someone might think I had come to murder them and smash a pot over my head. Thankfully, Barnabas left an encouraging note right under the "Do Not Disturb" sign. So I followed him to Peter's house.'

'Just as you expected, Uncle, of course,' John-Mark said,

looking more relaxed than he had done in a very long time.

Barnabas smiled. It had been a good day. He had solved a mystery, found a missing person and helped some very scared friends. Over supper he had been puzzling something else out too. What would become of Saul now? He surely couldn't go back to his old job of arresting Christians. And he had an amazing story to tell.

He would call it: 'The Case of the Damascus Road Murderer'.

Barnabas finished his supper, turned to Saul and smiled. 'I want to introduce you to some friends of mine,' he said. 'Let me tell you about a small Mediterranean island called Cyprus ...'

You can read all about Barnabas and Saul's adventures in Cyprus in Acts 13. And read how the Bible tells this story in Acts 9.

LYDIA

THE TALE OF THE GROUNDBREAKING GREEK WHO MEANT BUSINESS

WELCOME TO GREECE

Greece is the birthplace of many exciting mythological heroes. Perhaps you have read about the incredible feats of Hercules, the battle wins of Odysseus or the courage of Atlanta. These stories began as cultural lessons in hope, strength and courage that adults passed on to children in ancient Greece and are still being enjoyed today.

There are true stories from Greece that are just as exciting. The following one took place in Northern Greece and has also been passed down through the generations to help people find hope, strength and courage in God. It features two missionaries, a fashion tycoon, a riot and an earthquake.

Lydia's market stall bustled from dawn to dusk, with rich people, super-rich people and the servants of crazy-rich people all queuing up to purchase the latest trends. Nobody left empty-handed. Lydia prided herself on her great products, her great customer relations and her great advertising slogans.

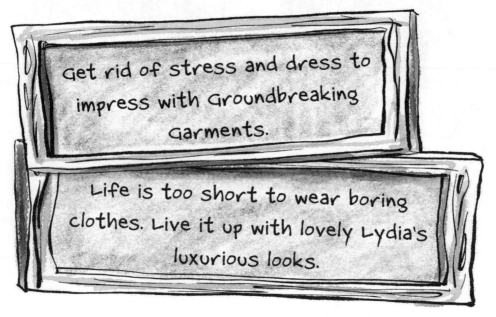

Get rid of stress and dress to impress with Groundbreaking Garments.

Life is too short to wear boring clothes. Live it up with lovely Lydia's luxurious looks.

The other market traders eyed Lydia with envy. She always had 10 times as many customers who paid 10 times more for each item sold. While they lived downtown in small, cramped houses, Lydia lived in a most desirable part of Philippi in a huge house. And, of course, she was always the best-dressed woman in the square.

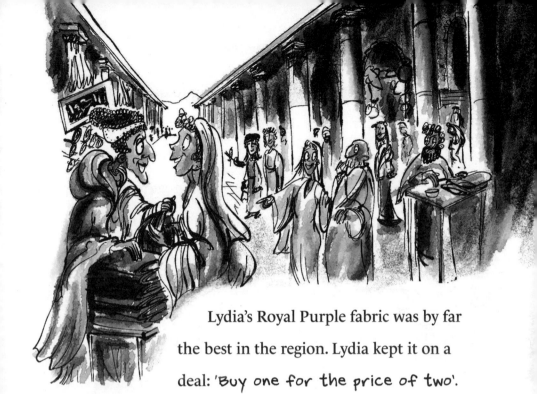

Lydia's Royal Purple fabric was by far the best in the region. Lydia kept it on a deal: 'Buy one for the price of two'.

It sold so well that she even earned a place on the famous Great Guild of Purple Pigment Dyers. It was no mean feat getting a place on the Great Guild of Purple Pigment Dyers – especially for a woman. But Lydia wasn't just an ordinary Greek woman of the first century: she featured in Philippi's top 10 businesspeople of the year. Every year. It was no wonder people flocked to her stall.

Even though Lydia was rich and successful, even though she was on the cutting edge of fashion, even though she worked hard and loved her job, even though she lived in a huge house, something was missing from her life.

Lydia's personal assistant Justus swept in one morning with the new slogan rolling off his tongue. **'If you dress happy, you will be happy.'**

'I **just** wanted to check. I'm **just** putting it on our marketing boards **just** for next week.' Justus' overuse of the word **just** was **just** something you **just** had to get used to.

'Are you happy to **just** sign it off? **Just** for me?'

'Am I happy to sign it off?' Lydia echoed back, deep in thought. 'Am I happy …? Am I really happy? I'm sorry, Justus, but I don't think we can use this. It's not strictly true.'

'Well, that's never stopped us before. **Just** remember …'

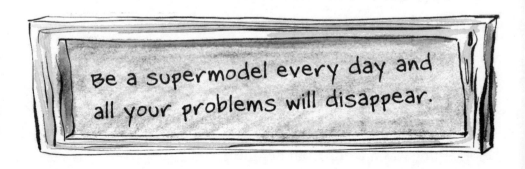

Be a supermodel every day and all your problems will disappear.

> The power of purple: popularity guaranteed.

Lydia laughed. Justus was very good at making her laugh. She was happy most of the time, but still something was missing. What was it? She exercised. She had friends. She'd even tried religion.

'**Just** a minute! You went where?' Justus asked, when she'd got back one morning.

'To the Jewish women's prayer meeting,' Lydia replied as she inspected the latest batch of fabrics.

'**Just** like that? Whatever for?'

'To pray of course!' Lydia said.

'**Just** the same – why the Jewish group? It's not like we haven't got gods and goddesses **just** right here in Greece!'

Justus knew everything there was to know about Greek mythology. He reeled off a few deities Lydia might like:

'There's Zeus – the god of the sky – just a bit Zeus-less if you need help on dry ground.

There's Hard-to-Miss Artemis – just in case you need a goddess of hunting.

There's Achilles – but he can be just such a pain in the ankle.

There's Hebe – goddess of youth – just she gives me the jeebies.

... And four hundred or so others. **Just** take your pick.'

Lydia knew that being a member of the Jewish women's prayer meeting was not something Greek tycoons were supposed to do, but she kept going anyway. There was one particular poem they used to read from time to time that made her think she somehow belonged there. The poem was called *The Woman of Noble Character* and celebrated the skills of a businesswoman like her who traded garments, wore purple and trusted God.

'What's going on?' Lydia whispered to one of the women one morning. She had arrived late to find two men at the women's prayer meeting. 'I didn't think they were allowed.'

'Not loud enough?' said the shorter of the two men. 'Shall I speak up? I was talking about the long-awaited Messiah.'

The taller man said nothing.

'The women ... of this group ... for women,' Lydia said sharply, 'are perfectly capable of waiting for the Messiah without your assistance.'

'Sisters,' the short man repeated, 'you'll find the Messiah has arrived! He has saved us! Repent and believe the good news, sisters, and you will find eternal happiness!'

Lydia rolled her eyes. The man sounded like the advertising slogans she used last year.

Feeling frumpy?
Fashion will save you!

Make an everlasting impression
with Groundbreaking Garments!

Lydia wondered what these men were really selling. She knew enough about business to understand there was no such thing as a free gift. On the other hand, she wasn't one to miss out on a bargain – if there really was eternal happiness, she meant to get hold of it.

So she came up with a plan.

That night, she served dinner to the whole of the Jewish **women's** prayer group and the two **men** that had gate-crashed.

The short man was called Paul. He walked with a limp, and when he talked, his thick, bushy eyebrows moved up and down. His nose protruded at a slight angle, which made him look like he'd been in a fight or two. But what mainly stood out about Paul was the way he talked about Jesus – as though he were actually there in the room with him.

Silas, the taller man, was more of the silent type. He seemed to be permanently praying. Lydia was afraid to talk to him, in case she interrupted something important.

By the end of the meal, Lydia knew she had found the thing that was missing from her life. This Jesus that Paul talked about sounded even more inspiring than the Woman of Noble Character. He fed the hungry, healed the sick, welcomed the poor, died on the cross, rose from the dead, fulfilled all the prophets said about him, helped the church with his Spirit, and called people everywhere to join his family.

But there was one thing bothering her. 'Paul, I can't stop thinking about Jesus on the cross. You said the Romans tortured him with a crown of thorns on his head, and put a purple robe round his shoulders. Do you think ...' Lydia stuttered, 'that the purple robe they used was one of mine?'

Lydia felt terrible. To think that a robe that may have been dyed in her warehouse, stitched in her home and sold on her stall to a passing Roman could then be used to torture the Messiah! She could hardly bear the shame of it. What if the outfit she was wearing was cut from the very same cloth? She couldn't stand to look at herself.

'I know exactly how you feel,' Paul admitted. 'I used to be known as Saul the Slaughterer, famous for arresting Christians and watching them die slowly. But if Jesus can forgive me, he can forgive you too and take away your shame.'

One by one, everyone in Lydia's household began to remember things they had said, done or thought that had added to Jesus' suffering.

One by one, everyone asked Jesus for forgiveness.

One by one, Paul and Silas baptised them as Christians.

'The old has gone. The new is here!' he said as they came out of the water.

'Clothe yourselves with compassion,' Paul said as he blessed them.

Lydia was beginning to realise that Paul's words were not just slick slogans and empty promises like her adverts. They were the real deal.

'I **just** think you're crazy,' Justus said a few days later. 'Your Christianity thing will **just** be so bad for business. People will boycott our stall. **Just** you wait and see!'

'I know, Justus, but it's a small sacrifice. And we've still got the best Royal Purple outfits in town!'

'Can you at least get the new church to **just** move out of your house? It must be time for Paul and Silas to move on by now?'

'They're not staying with me tonight, Justus,' Lydia said sadly. 'They've been thrown in prison. For trying to help a slave girl. Apparently, they've been beaten badly. I'm going to see what can be done in the morning.'

Some mornings come quicker than others. This one would be a long time coming.

In the middle of that night, Lydia's dark room began moving as though it had been dropped onto a boat in the middle of a stormy ocean. The vase by her bed slid onto the floor and smashed. She heard crashes from the kitchen and screams outside and she darted under a table to hide.

It was not the first time Lydia had woken up to an earthquake, but this one seemed more violent than any she had ever experienced.

When the rumbles stopped, Lydia saw that although her house and everyone in it was safe, her neighbours had not been so lucky.

Lydia did not rush to rescue her fabrics like she had after the earthquake the year before. Instead, for the rest of the night, she helped to pull people out of the rubble. Her many spare rooms, and her many, many spare clothes were soon being put to good use. She was even making people smile with her new slogans.

Groundbreaking Garments —
what's mine is yours.

Free for all — no terms
and conditions apply.

There was one thing left to do. When the choking dust died down, Lydia ran into what remained of the town. As she looked around in the moonlight, it was as she feared. At the old prison building, ceilings had caved in, doors were hanging off on their hinges and the walls had huge holes in them. Paul and Silas were nowhere to be found.

Lydia cried all the way home.

Lydia's house was now a hive of activity – not only filled with her household and her work colleagues but with a large number of homeless, hungry people dressed in her trademark Royal Purple, and with every Christian in Philippi praying for one another.

It was so noisy that nobody heard the knock on the door at first.

Knock, knock.

Knock, KNOCK!

'Lydia!' Justus called. '**Just** look! A whole legion of Roman guards and officials are here. I **just knew** you shouldn't have invited strangers into your home. What is the point of surviving an earthquake one night **just** to face execution the next?'

Lydia prayed that she would be as brave as Paul and Silas had been. She took a deep breath and opened the door wide.

'Come in. All of you! Welcome!'

'Err … we are returning your guests, madam.' The man in charge seemed strangely embarrassed. 'We are sorry for any inconvenience.'

'My guests?'

The large crowd of soldiers turned and left leaving two remarkably familiar faces standing on her doorstep.

'Paul? Silas? You're alive! But how? I thought … we all thought … you were dead! Did you escape during the earthquake?'

'We could have escaped,' Paul said, squeezing into the crowded house. 'But we were too busy telling the other prisoners about Jesus.'

Silas chuckled to himself.

'He's remembering the poor prison guard,' Paul explained. 'He thought we had escaped. He was about to kill himself.'

'That's not funny!' Lydia said.

'No, but you should have seen his face when we all

appeared! First, he was relieved we hadn't escaped. Then he was terrified we were about to kill him!'

'**Just** a second! You **just** chose to **just** stay in prison?!' Justus just couldn't believe what he was hearing.

'Yes, but we did all nip back to the guard's house for an hour or so for food and bandages. After he had become a Christian, that is.'

Lydia and Justus both looked most surprised. 'Your prison guard – became a Christian?'

'And his whole family! He had us back safe in our crumbled cells by morning.'

'Tell me you're **just** kidding,' Justus said.

'It's all true. And then the magistrates appeared and apologised for imprisoning us without a trial.'

Lydia could hardly believe it. 'What a night of shocks!'

'Socks?' Paul asked. 'Yes please. Actually, I think we could really do with a whole new outfit! Do you have anything we could borrow?'

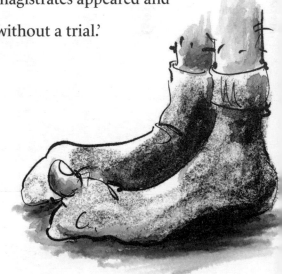

'Groundbreaking Garments: style that shocks,' Justus laughed. **'Just** wait until I get that onto the marketing board!'

Lydia smiled. She loved being a businesswoman, but following Jesus was an adventure like none other.

'Just one more thing,' Justus said, with one last surprise up his sleeve for Lydia. 'It's **just** your God sounds very different to our Greek gods. So, I was **just** thinking, can I **just** come along to your church **just** this evening – **just** to find out a little bit more?'

You can read this story in Acts 16. Lydia's favourite poem, *The Woman of Noble Character*, is also in the Bible (Proverbs 31). If you want to find out what happens to Lydia's church, you could read the letter Paul wrote to the Philippians a few years later when he was chained up in prison – again!

ONESIMUS

THE TALE OF THE TURKISH TRUANT
WHO RISKED EVERYTHING

WELCOME TO TURKEY

Turkey is a beautiful country that bridges Europe and Asia.
It is famous for bringing the world delicious treats such as
kebabs, Turkish delight and chocolate spread.

Much of Turkey still looks as it would have done 2000
years ago: the beautiful coastline studded with islands,
the mountains and foothills with their dazzling lakes and

outcrops, bustling towns and waterways, and reminders of
ancient civilisations.

When the hero of this story began his long-distance
hike through Turkey, he did not have time to admire the
scenery. But the world around him was about to change,
and it was partly due to his brave decision.

'Wrong again, Onesimus!'

'Not like that, Onesimus!'

'I said no, Onesimus!'

'Oh no, Onesimus!'

'NOOOOOO!!'

Oh-**no**-simus this. Oh-**no**-simus that. His nickname reminded him every day that he was not just a slave but a clumsy, careless, good-for-**no**thing slave.

In his dreams, everything was different.

In his dreams, Onesimus the Almighty Slave Driver told Master Philemon what to do.

'Mow the lawns with your teeth, **dirtbag!**'

'Peel those onions until your eyeballs fall out, **cry baby!**'

'Cut my toenails and eat them for breakfast, **slimeball!**'

All night, he was the master of his own fate, but when he woke up, he found himself back at the bottom of the heap, the lowest of all the lowly slaves.

By day, he had to clean out Philemon's stinking animals. He had to help prepare food for Philemon's fat guests while he himself was starving hungry. He had to put sheets on Philemon's bed while Philemon sat around all day doing nothing.

And then

he had to do it all again because, of course, 'Oh-no-simus' had done it all wrong! The chief slave scolded him and laughed at him and scolded him some more.

On Friday nights came another form of torture. All the slaves were locked away, and a crowd of visitors were welcomed in. From his pile of straw in the corner of the barn, Onesimus could hear them laughing and singing about their freedom:

'If the Son sets you free,
you will be free indeed.'

It was like lemon juice being squeezed into his sore eyes, and salt being rubbed into his blistered hands at the same time.

Onesimus tried many different ways of blocking out the cruel music.

He tried singing 'Blah blah blah' at the top of his voice.

He tried standing on his head until he heard loud ringing in his ears.

He even stole chicken livers from the kitchen and shoved them in his earholes.

Nothing worked.

Onesimus toasted the stolen earwax-marinated chicken livers on the fire and ate them. That was a mistake. Not only could he still hear the torture music, he could also hear the other slaves doing chicken impressions behind his back.

'Oh-**no**-simus – useless slave for sale – going **cheep!**'

'Oh-**no**-simus just doesn't have the **guts** for it.'

'Oh-**no**-simus is going to feel **offal** tomorrow when they brand him as a thief.'

'Oh-**no**-simus will have to **live-r** with the scars forever.'

It was the last straw. He had no doubt that the chief slaves would report his theft. And he knew that thieves got the word **'thief'** burned into their foreheads with a hot branding iron. His only choice was to try to run away. If he got caught, which he probably would, the punishment would be even worse.

But perhaps, if he was really lucky, he could get a little taste of the freedom he longed for.

When all the other slaves had fallen asleep, Onesimus dug a hole under the barn, crawled out into the gardens, crept to the edge of the lawns, leapt over the wall and disappeared into the night.

First, he felt exhilarated – anywhere had to be better than Philemon's house, even the spooky, dark woods.

Then he felt terrified – he had no food, no money, no plan, no sense of direction and nowhere to go. He had nothing to protect himself against the wild animals.

Then he felt even more terrifyingly terrified. The slave-catchers loved the chase more than the reward and were probably already under orders to bring the runaway back alive or dead.

Day 1: Woods

Distance travelled: 10 kilometres.

Food eaten: two earwax-covered chicken livers.

Memorable moment: hiding inside a wolf carcass to avoid slave-catchers.

Day 2: Hills

Distance travelled: 20 kilometres.

Food eaten: two apples stolen from an orchard.

Memorable moment: falling out of an apple tree.

Day 3: Valleys

Distance travelled: 25 kilometres.

Food eaten: half a rotten fish.

Memorable moment: regurgitating half of a rotten fish.

Day 4: River

Distance travelled: not much.

Food eaten: nothing

Memorable moment: none.

Onesimus was so tired and hungry he couldn't go one step further. He lay down in a ditch and began to dream of life as a slave. At least at Philemon's house he had a roof over his head and food that stayed down. At least there, someone occasionally talked to him, even if was just to say …

'Oi!'

'OI! YOU!'

Onesimus woke to a large boot in his face. If he could have jumped up and run away, he would have jumped up and run away.

'You! Eat this!' said the man attached to the boot, tossing him some dry bread. 'When you're done, unload my boat onto the bank. If anyone sees you, scarper. And don't say you saw me. Or you'll end up sleeping at the bottom of the river.'

For the next few weeks, Onesimus went from one dodgy job to another. Each was worse than the one before. When he saw a large boat laden high with crates one evening, he took his chance and jumped on board.

Now he was a runaway and a stowaway.

Day 20: Spice Boat

Distance travelled: 50 kilometres.

Food eaten: chilli powder sandwich.

Memorable moment: making rats sneeze with black pepper.

Day 30: Wine Boat

Distance travelled: 40 kilometres.

Food eaten: captain's leftovers.

Memorable moment: spooking drunken sailors.

Day 36: Prison Ship

Distance travelled: 40 kilometres.

Food eaten: don't ask.

Memorable moment: being spotted by a crewmate but mistaken for a corpse.

You might have thought that after such a long journey Onesimus was getting used to his freedom. But he wasn't. He knew that at any minute he could get caught and killed. He'd been on the run for almost two months and was hundreds of miles away from Philemon's house, but he was just as scared and sad as ever.

When the prison ship stopped in a large city, Onesimus managed to slip off and into a side street without being spotted. He grabbed some rotting vegetables left by one of the docks and scampered away. He had to find somewhere safe to hide until morning. Then, if he was lucky, he would sneak aboard another ship.

Just then, he heard something torturous. He felt mad. And terrified. Someone was singing at the top of their voice:

*'If the Son sets you free,
you will be free indeed.'*

'Stop!' Onesimus burst out, before he could stop himself. He picked up some mouldy pomegranates from a discarded crate and launched them into the shadows.

Splat. Splat. SPLAT.

The singing stopped.

'God bless you, brother!' a voice said.

Suddenly, two dock guards appeared. Onesimus leapt into the shadows.

He held his breath as the guards passed by. The singer had gone silent too. That's when he noticed a low window next to him with bars. Behind the bars was a basement. Chained to the basement wall was a strange little man. His mouth was dripping with red juice. Around his feet, six enormous, fat cockroaches were fighting over discarded pomegranate skins.

'God bless you, brother!' the little man said, holding out his hand and letting a cockroach climb up his arm. 'Do you need a place to stay?'

Onesimus had slept in many unimaginably bad places recently, but he refused to even consider sharing a stinking basement with a weird singing prisoner and his pet creepy crawlies.

'This city is dangerous at night. Go stay with the dove lady. Tell her Paul sent you in return for the pomegranates. God bless you and keep you safe.'

Onesimus had no intention of staying with the dove lady either. He didn't trust anyone any more.

That night was the worst night of his whole life.

First, he ran from the dock guards, then a pack of wild dogs, then a plague of rats, then more dock guards, then his own shadow, then the worst of the city's criminal underworld. Every hiding place was occupied by something even more frightful than the last.

Just when Onesimus was about to give up, he spotted six white doves in the moonlight flapping up and down on a wall.

Before he could think twice, Onesimus leapt over the wall and landed in a compost heap on the other side. A hundred doves flew up in the air in surprise before gently landing all around him. Onesimus didn't move. He had never seen anything so beautiful.

'Can I help you?' said an old lady. Her voice sounded scared, but also kind. 'Did Paul send you?'

The woman hobbled towards the compost heap. For the first time in a long time Onesimus didn't run away.

Over the next few weeks, Onesimus began to feel more like a human being than ever before in his life. He had a real bed to sleep in, warm food on a plate and someone to talk to. Each morning he planned to leave again, but the dove lady always persuaded him to stay just one more night, to get his strength up. She always needed him to take just one more package to Paul.

Every evening, Onesimus
took these packages and posted
them through the basement
window. Sometimes they
contained food. Sometimes pen
and paper. Sometimes letters.
Onesimus even began to enjoy
listening to Paul's peculiar
stories.

'Can I ask you something?'
Onesimus asked one day. 'You
sing a lot of songs, but there
is one particular one … about
being free indeed.'

'If the Son sets you free ...' Paul began to sing.

'My slave master Philemon used to sing that song before I ran away,' Onesimus interrupted. 'It drove me mad. How could he sing about his freedom while not caring about mine? Now you sing about freedom while being chained up. It doesn't make sense.'

'Philemon and I both know we are free on the inside,' Paul explained. 'Free from guilt and shame. You can't help singing about that sort of freedom. But you are right – I think there's more to the freedom Jesus taught than Philemon may have realised.'

Onesimus wished he could tear away the bars and break the chains and give Paul a hug.

The next evening, when Onesimus delivered a package to Paul, Paul had something for Onesimus too. With tears in his eyes, he handed over a letter.

'Would you please deliver it for me? God bless you, brother.'

Onesimus saw the name on the front of the letter and his heart sank. But he understood. If Paul could trust God trapped in prison, then Onesimus could trust God trapped in slavery. It was time to turn himself in.

Nobody saw the boy jumping on board a prison ship in the middle of the night. He found a place to hide and prayed it was going back the way it came.

A few weeks later, the wine ship was spotted unloading on the docks. It was loaded back up with empty barrels and a small stowaway recognised only by the rats.

Just when the stowaway thought he would die of starvation, he saw land. He jumped off, swam to the bank, grabbed some food and found a hiding place on the spice dock.

A few days later, the boat pulled in alongside a ditch the boy had once slept in.

He waited for nightfall before following the valley up into the hills.

The next night, he passed a familiar-looking orchard.

The night after that, he spotted a rotten wolf skeleton and then, finally, a low wall he hadn't seen for almost six months.

Now all Onesimus had to do was post the letter and then …

'Well, look who it is!'

Onesimus knew that sneering voice only two well. He felt two strong arms squeezing him tightly across his chest. He couldn't move.

'Oh-**no**-simus! You can't even run away properly, can you? I thought the slave-catchers would bring you back. But now the reward is mine!'

It all came flooding back. The cruelty of the other slaves that matched the cruelty of Philemon. He was suddenly Oh-**no**-simus again. The good-for-**no**thing, **no**-hoper with **no** friends. He was dragged into Philemon's house and shoved to the ground at his master's feet. The chief slave who had caught him stood back looking very pleased with himself.

'**YOU?!**' Philemon spat over the boy cowering on the ground. 'Do you know how much time and money has been wasted hunting for you? Do you? You're a disgrace.'

'Please sir?' Onesimus tried to remember what he had once planned to say if he ever saw Philemon again.

'Don't you **"please sir"** me.' Philemon scowled. 'I don't want to do this, but you give me no choice.' He turned to the chief slave who was enjoying watching Onesimus squirm in fear. 'Bring me the branding iron, and make sure it's hot. **Burning hot.**'

'But sir, I have a **letter** for you.' Onesimus reached quickly into his pocket and dropped the letter at Philemon's feet. 'It's from Paul.'

At the mention of Paul's name, Philemon took a step back and gave Onesimus a strange look. Slowly he bent down, picked up the letter and broke the seal.

Philemon loomed over Onesimus as he read the letter.

The chief slave appeared and loomed beside him holding the hot branding iron.

Onesimus braced himself.

Philemon pounced on him. It took Onesimus a second or two to realise this wasn't an attack at all – it was an embrace!

'Onesimus – I'm **so sorry,**' Philemon said.

'I understand now. It's like Paul says. You are not a slave to be punished – you are a **brother to be welcomed**.'

The chief slave dropped the burning hot branding iron in surprise. It landed on his toes with a hiss, and he ran out of the room crying like a baby.

Onesimus woke up to a busy day ahead. There was work to be done: animals to clean out, beds to make, food to prepare, lawns to be tidied.

'Your turn to peel the onions too,' continued the chief slave. 'And don't forget – it's Friday! You know what that means!'

'Oh yes!' Onesimus whooped.

He smiled. It was no wonder the other slaves had started calling him 'Oh-yes-imus'.

Oh yes.

Today he would work but tonight he would celebrate. Together with Philemon and the other Christians in the area, rich and poor, male and female, old and young, slave and free, he would raise his voice and sing the song he loved most in the whole world:

> *'If the Son sets you free,*
> *you will be free indeed.'*

You can read the letter Paul sent back with Onesimus. It is towards the end of your Bible and is called 'Philemon'. It may be a very short letter but it changed history. Because Onesimus took the risk of his life in delivering that letter, Christians everywhere know that God wants us to treat one another with dignity and help free those caught in slavery.

ACKNOWLEDGEMENTS

I should be more careful about what I complain about! Bemoaning the lack of international heroes in children's books as an aside in a sermon one day, I had no idea that my friend Ruth Roff was listening. Ruth had been newly charged as commissioning editor to publish books exploring the Bible through stories for children – and she turned my complaint into a challenge: to create something that celebrated the diversity seen in the Bible. Meanwhile my wife Miriam, who had been writing some children's stories for fun during the lockdown of 2020, accepted the challenge on our behalf.

Thank you so much Ruth, not only for the challenge but also for helping steer us onward – from the concept stage to the finished manuscript. It has been a lot of fun and you have introduced us to some fantastic people on the way. Thank you Andy Gray for those amazing impressive illustrations that have really made our stories come alive. Thank you David Gatward for your very useful masterclass on writing for children. Thank you Jessica Lacey for your excellent editing and pulling everything together at the end. Thank you Zoe Willis for your rigorous research for the artwork, and Natalie Chen for your ambitious art direction. Thank you Jo Stockdale for the comprehensive copyedit and Helen Jones for the profound proofread. You have all been brilliant!

A particular thank you to our nephews and nieces who laughed at all the jokes and gasped at all the action – and occasionally corrected our spelling. Finally, thank you to all of you children we have had the privilege to help raise – you have taught us how to see the Bible through your eyes, asking all sorts of questions that have really made us think and wonder, and wonder some more.

ABOUT THE AUTHORS

Dr Krish Kandiah is a theologian, author and activist, and works with the government to improve the lives of vulnerable children in the care system. He and his wife, Miriam, are birth parents, adoptive parents and foster carers and are passionate about helping children to flourish. Together they have authored fourteen books.

ABOUT THE ILLUSTRATOR

Andy has been drawing for as long as he can remember. He's also a DJ, producer, speaker, magician, and even a Church of England minister. He's worked professionally with children and young people for over thirty years in schools and churches. Sometimes he gets bored. He is proud to be autistic and encourages people to embrace their uniqueness and live life to the full.

Hodder & Stoughton is the UK's leading Christian publisher with a wide range of books from the bestselling authors in the UK and around the world. Having published Bibles and Christian books for more than 150 years, Hodder & Stoughton are delighted to launch Hodder Faith Young Explorers – a list of books for children.

Join us on this new adventure!

Visit **www.hodderfaithyoungexplorers.co.uk** to find out more.